RAISED ROW GARDENING

RAISED ROW GARDENING

INCREDIBLE ORGANIC PRODUCE WITH NO TILLING AND MINIMAL WEEDING

JIM & MARY COMPETTI
FOUNDERS OF OLD WORLD GARDEN FARMS

First published in 2018 by
Page Street Publishing Co.
27 Congress Street, Suite 105
Salem, MA 01970
www.pagestreetpublishing.com

Distributed by Macmillan, sales in Canada by The Canadian Manda Group.

22 21 20 19 18 1 2 3 4 5

ISBN-13: 978-1-62414-494-3
ISBN-10: 1-62414-494-2

Library of Congress Control Number: 2017956342

Cover and book design by Page Street Publishing Co.
Photography by Erica Kay
Illustrations by Jade Gedeon

Printed and bound in the United States

THIS BOOK IS DEDICATED TO OUR BELOVED AND FAITHFUL FOLLOWERS OF OLD WORLD GARDEN FARMS

Our creation and love of Raised Row Gardening, and the quest for a more fulfilling and simpler way to garden has been nurtured, questioned, broadened and honed by your constant companionship. Without you, this book would never have been possible. Thank you for inspiring and pushing us to heights we could never have imagined.

Happy gardening!

CONTENTS

OWG
OWG
OWG

old world
GARDEN
FARMS

INTRODUCTION

What if gardening could truly be fun? Although there are tens of millions of gardeners around the world who are incredibly passionate about growing their own food, you would be hard-pressed to find more than a handful that wouldn't agree that it can be physically challenging at times.

What if gardening didn't need to consist of backbreaking work? What if you didn't have to spend hour upon hour digging, hoeing, tilling and weeding your garden to end up with wonderful, delicious and healthy vegetables? What if you could create an organic, naturally sustainable garden that could produce a harvest beyond your wildest imagination, with as little as ten minutes of garden work each day?

Sound impossible? Well, it's not! Using our Raised Row Gardening method, which we have developed and refined over the last seven years, gardening becomes simple, inexpensive, extremely rewarding and, most importantly, downright fun.

OUR VERY FIRST RAISED ROW GARDEN

On a wide open, 20 by 40 foot (6 by 12 meter) grassy knoll on a rolling hillside, with nothing more than a few ordinary garden tools, we created our first Raised Row Garden from scratch in the spring of 2011. There was no plow, no rototiller, and for that matter, no power equipment to speak of at all.

We built our first Raised Row Garden directly on top of the grass. We used simple, inexpensive and locally available organic straw, topsoil and compost to create our first growing rows. To help suppress weeds, we used a thick layer of straw and leaves to cover the open walking spaces between the rows.

All in all, that first garden cost $125 to create, and the majority of that cost was from a load of topsoil brought in to build the raised earthen rows. We planted the garden in late May, and held our breath in hopes of a mid-summer harvest.

And what a harvest it was! The garden flourished. To say we were blown away with the results that first year would be an understatement. That little plot of open land, with just eleven raised growing rows, provided over 2,500 pounds (1,100 kg) of vegetables. We harvested more than forty bushels of tomatoes by the end of August, and in one single picking, hauled in six bushels of peppers. Cucumbers, potatoes, green beans, sugar snap peas and zucchini filled the harvest baskets as well. That first year, we canned over 250 jars of pasta sauce, salsa, tomato juice, pepper rings, relish, pickles, beans and more. Best of all, and much to our relief, our Raised Row Garden didn't require huge amounts of labor to plant or maintain. In fact, we spent an average of just ten minutes a day to keep the garden virtually weed-free. It became blatantly apparent at the end of that very first year that our makeshift Raised Row Garden didn't just work—it worked amazingly well!

We have come a long way from that first garden, experimenting, trialing and refining the Raised Row Garden method year after year. It has truly evolved into a revolutionary new garden system that allows gardeners of any age the opportunity to grow more of their family's food without the time, expense and workload that traditional gardening methods can take.

Chapter by chapter, this book will take you through the steps and stages of gardening the Raised Row way. From first-year setup to planting, harvesting and maintaining an incredibly productive garden year after year.

From the novice gardener to the experienced grower, Raised Row Gardening is an excellent way to enjoy the passion for growing vegetables without the stress, strain, cost and labor that so many gardeners fear.

Mary Competti

BEANS

CHAPTER 1

THE GARDEN THAT STARTED A RAISED ROW CRAZE

One of the most common complaints among gardeners young and old is the amount of labor and time required to build and maintain a productive vegetable garden. In a traditional garden setup, that workload starts with the tilling chores of spring. And that, of course, can only occur if the soil is dry enough to work. Next come the constant, laborious chores of weeding, hoeing, raking and re-tilling rows over and over.

It's a vicious cycle of endless work that can turn the most enthusiastic gardener into a defeated soul. For many, by mid-summer, the garden has become a weedy, tangled, overrun mixture of vegetables and marauding insects that have combined to form a backyard eyesore, and a disheartened gardener.

And that is exactly where we were some seven-plus years ago. Defeated. We loved the concept of growing our own food and providing fresh, organic vegetables to our kids. But with two active careers, and four growing children with a full slate of activities, we were hard pressed to devote the time and energy required to maintain a traditional garden. There had to be a better way that could work for our busy lives and us.

Up to that point, we had relied solely on the knowledge gleaned from traditional, mainstream, backyard vegetable gardening methods. Gardening knowledge that had been passed down from our parents and their parents.

We both came from families that loved to garden. We have incredibly fond memories of the amazing vegetables those gardens of yesteryear produced. There was nothing better as a child than biting into a just-picked, crisp cucumber, or sinking your teeth into the soft, juicy skin of a vine-ripened tomato. And who can forget sitting on the back porch snapping green beans and husking fresh sweet corn with Grandma, anticipating that wondrous homegrown feast that would be enjoyed by the whole family later that evening.

Those were the memories that drove us to want those same fresh, healthy and delicious vegetables for our own family. But sadly, it is also where the love affair of the past came to a screeching halt!

Unfortunately, those vegetable gardens of our parents required hours of hard labor to maintain. Those wondrous memories mentioned above were also filled with some not-so-fond memories of slogging through just-tilled mud and filling bucket after bucket with weeds. Adding to the agony, we knew we would be re-drafted a few days later to repeat the same miserable tasks all over again.

It was those haunting memories that left us searching for how to grow our own food without re-living that horrifying portion of our childhood. One thing was for sure. A traditional garden created by plowing, tilling, raking, hoeing and re-tilling soil throughout the entire growing season was not going to be the answer for us. Let's look at the different types of garden setups to better understand the differences.

TRADITIONAL PLOWED / TILLED GARDEN

In a traditional plowed / tilled garden, it all starts with breaking up the soil. This can take multiple hours and several passes with a plow, tiller or a combination of both to prepare the space for planting. Whether you own or rent, it also requires a sizeable financial investment in the required equipment, such as a tractor, plow and rototiller, along with the fuel needed to power them.

Traditional gardening is also extremely weather dependent. One must wait until the soil has properly dried out to plow and till. If not, the soil can quickly become clumped and unworkable, leaving a garden space that is less than ideal for planting.

To make it even more difficult, the tilling process must be completed several times to break up the soil enough for planting. And in a traditional garden setup, of course, this work must take place at the beginning of EVERY single year!

RAISED BED GARDEN

Raised beds utilize man-made or natural materials to create an elevated growing space in which plants are grown. Although raised beds have many advantages over a traditional tilled garden, they can certainly be quite time-consuming and costly to create and maintain.

First, there is the wood, stone, metal or plastic required to build the permanent borders. It can be quite expensive to purchase, and can take a lot of time to construct and fill with soil. Depending on the materials chosen, those "permanent borders" also may need to be replaced every so often, adding to the cost of the raised bed system.

The soil in a raised bed must be replaced or amended annually with compost and/or fertilizers to keep its strength and vitality. This can be difficult depending on the style of bed created. If soil is to be turned over, or amendments need to be added, the border material can get in the way, making it difficult to work with a shovel.

RAISED ROW GARDEN

Raised rows utilize many of the concepts and advantages of raised beds, without the hassle and expense of building borders. Instead of outlining each planting area with expensive materials, the soil in a Raised Row Garden slightly tapers down to form a natural, earthen edge on each side of the growing row.

This natural sloping edge does more than just save on the cost of materials and labor needed to form bed space. As you will see later, it also helps immensely with the ease of long-term maintenance and productivity.

The soil in a Raised Row Garden never needs to be replaced. It can be easily amended to not only maintain its fertility, but also to improve upon it with each subsequent growing season. The borderless nature of the Raised Row Garden also makes it easy to incorporate all types of organic and sustainable materials back into the soil, including compost, natural fertilizers and, most importantly, cover crops.

All of these factors combine to truly make the Raised Row Garden method the most economical and productive choice for home produce gardening.

THE PITFALLS OF TRADITIONAL GARDENING—THE PLOW AND ROTOTILLER

Somewhere along the line, plowing, tilling and "working" the soil became the accepted norm for how to create a backyard garden. Whether it was the mechanized ease of breaking up hard ground, or the seemingly perfect tidy path of crumbled earth left behind the wake of a rototiller's tracks, tilling and repeatedly digging up the soil was thought to be the way to start and maintain a vegetable garden.

Unfortunately, the entire process of "working the soil" time and time again creates more expense and effort for the gardener, and less than ideal growing conditions for the soil.

The action of tilling a garden causes much more harm than good. Tilling replants dormant weed seeds from the top layer of soil, and can destroy soil structure over time.

Why Tilling Is Not the Answer

Over time, a garden's soil structure and fertility can be damaged and depleted by the constant act of plowing, tilling and digging. Soil, in its natural, undisturbed state, contains a vital network of organic and life-giving materials and organisms. This includes everything from layers of humus, to beneficial compounds and minerals, worms, insects and microorganisms. The soil's structure also contains naturally occurring air pockets that stand ready to deliver needed oxygen below to a plant's root system.

Every time soil is tilled, this entire network is compromised. As the beneficial compounds and microorganisms are brought to the surface, they dry out and die from the exposure. Air pockets are eliminated, replaced and filled in by the crushed grains of the tilled soil. Tilling simply destroys the natural harmony of soil, all the while contributing to an explosion of weeds, one of the biggest problems all gardeners face.

It is ironic that although many use a rototiller to turn under existing weeds to both prepare and maintain a garden, this can actually exasperate the problem by creating more weeds than were present before.

Thousands upon thousands of perennial and annual weed seeds are spread by wind, birds and other wildlife. These seeds lay on the surface of the soil, waiting to find an opportunity to grow. Tilling provides them that opportunity and then some. Every time a garden is tilled, weed seeds at the surface are incorporated into the soil below, giving them the perfect growing medium for germination and survival. With each successive tilling, more and more weeds find the perfect home to wreak havoc upon your garden.

THE BIRTH OF THE RAISED ROW GARDEN METHOD

So, what really was the best way for us to garden? We looked at nearly every viable option we could find, including raised bed, square foot gardening, hydroponic, the double-dig French method, bio-intensive gardening, container gardening and everything in between.

All of them had built-in advantages over traditional gardening methods in some way, shape or form. Yet, all had obvious drawbacks as well. Whether it was the cost of start-up, expensive tools or the time and labor involved to maintain the garden, none of the prior methods mentioned were going to create the kind of garden we dreamed of, wanted and needed.

What was that dream garden? A garden that would use natural, organic, sustainable materials and methods to produce safe, healthy and abundant food, all while requiring little investment in the tools, labor and time needed to maintain it to fit our busy lifestyle.

So, doing what humans have been doing for thousands of years, we looked to create a better way.

We took the best of the best of gardening methods, added in a multitude of our own soil-building, time-saving and inexpensive ideas and came up with a more efficient and effective way to garden. The Raised Row Gardening system was born.

A Raised Row Garden naturally eliminates 80% of garden maintenance by concentrating most of the effort in only the space where plants are grown.

The Raised Row approach puts an emphasis on disturbing the soil less, while concentrating efforts and resources in only the specific areas where plants will be grown. This, in turn, lessens the workload and expense to the gardener.

By utilizing a combination of mulch, compost and cover crops, and pinpointing their use, the Raised Row Gardening method increases and maintains the soil's fertility naturally and sustainably. In addition, with its constant mulching, it virtually eliminates weeds, and creates a garden that is productive and incredibly easy to maintain.

CHAPTER 2

CREATING YOUR VERY FIRST RAISED ROW GARDEN

At its very core, a Raised Row Garden is pure simplicity. The Raised Row Gardening method uses organic and sustainable practices to power a highly productive, low maintenance garden. As you will see in the coming chapters, it is not only simple to create, it's also simple to plant, and even easier to maintain.

More than anything else, the Raised Row method allows you to maximize yields while minimizing resources needed to grow your own food and the daily, weekly and annual maintenance chores. It also makes for an extremely neat and tidy garden space that is sure to be the envy of your friends, neighbors and fellow gardeners.

As with all gardens, the first year of setting up your Raised Row Garden will certainly be the most labor-intensive. However, the effort involved still pales in comparison to the workload, cost and potential downfalls of setting up the initial year using other popular gardening methods. In fact, once the first year is completed, the Raised Row Garden becomes increasingly easier to maintain with each successive season.

FACTORS TO CONSIDER BEFORE PLANTING A RAISED ROW GARDEN

Selecting the Location

Location, location, location! As with all gardens, finding the best and most suitable location for your Raised Row Garden will have a tremendous impact on its overall success. Avoid planting gardens in areas with too much shade, on steep slopes or in low-lying areas. Here are the keys when choosing the location for your Raised Row Garden.

Sunlight

A potential garden space that receives a minimum of six to eight hours of sunlight is ideal. Vegetable plants, just like many plants in nature, rely heavily on the process of photosynthesis to absorb the energy needed for strong growth and production. Too much shade leads to underdeveloped plants with significantly lower harvest yields.

In addition, sunlight helps to dry off plant foliage from rainfall and early morning dew, which is crucial in helping to prevent fungus, mildew and other moisture-related diseases.

That same sunlight also works to keep the soil from becoming too saturated after periods of heavy or extended rain. Although water is vital to a plant's survival, too much moisture at or below the surface of the soil can suffocate a plant's root system. When soil becomes waterlogged for extended periods of time, it forms a barrier around roots. This barrier keeps roots from being able to breath, depriving them of the oxygen needed for growth, and, ultimately, their survival.

To determine where the best and most available sunlight will be in your yard, spend a few days watching and documenting the sun's pattern. This will help you establish what spaces might work, and which need to be eliminated.

As you watch the sun's arc, take into consideration trees, buildings, fences and any potential obstructions that might keep plants from receiving the necessary amount of sunlight for good growth now and in the future. Consider all possibilities. If it's early spring, think about trees that might not yet have developed their full leaf canopy, which could later block sunlight. Consider the future growth of those trees, which may present a problem eventually.

Also consider what type of sunlight your garden will receive each day. At the end of the day, all sunlight is not equal when it comes to its effect on the growth and productivity of vegetable plants.

Choosing a garden site that receives six to eight hours of early morning to early afternoon sunlight is a much better choice than selecting one that receives only the hot, burning rays of mid-afternoon sunlight. Morning sunlight on a garden not only helps to dry off plants from overnight dew, keeping mildew and other disease at bay, but also it is less stressful to a vegetable plant's development. Scorching hot, midday and late-afternoon sunlight can cause extreme stress to plants, especially if it is the only sunlight they receive.

Avoiding Steep Slopes and Low-Lying Areas

By far, the best possible location to choose for your garden is a flat, level surface that is easily accessible. However, that is not always an option depending on the space you have available. Slight slopes with a drop of 3 feet (1 meter) or less for every 20 feet (6 meters) will work without much issue, but avoid areas with steeper slopes.

Steep slopes make it hard to have a consistent moisture level for your vegetable plants. With steep grades, rain and hand watering easily run off and away from root zones. This leads to little water for the plants at the top of the slope, and excessive moisture for those at the bottom.

Low-lying areas, on the other hand, become a major collection point for rainfall and runoff. As mentioned above, this can result in root suffocation, poor growth and, ultimately, plant failure.

This entire process of selecting the best location is vital to gardening success, and yet it is so often overlooked when initially determining the location of all types of gardens. But with a Raised Row Garden, that importance is heightened.

A Raised Row Garden, like fine wine, only gets better with time. Each successive year the soil becomes more enriched and productive. At the same time, garden issues such as weeds and pests, and the time and resources spent dealing with them, continue to decrease. Having to move your garden and start over in a few years because of a poor initial choice means losing those powerful advantages.

Soil Condition–One Thing You Don't Have to Worry About

The current fertility and vitality of the soil is not a make or break factor when choosing a location for your Raised Row Garden.

A Raised Row Garden, whether created from a previous garden space or built from scratch in a brand-new location, is built on top of the existing surface. Even if the existing soil below is rocky, clay-filled or sandy, the raised rows that will be built on top of the existing soil will provide plenty of nutrients for your plants to thrive.

Over time, that rich soil will also work its way into the soil surface directly below, creating an even better garden in the years to come.

With that said, if you do happen to be fortunate enough to have rich and fertile soil already in place, it can certainly be used in the initial process of building your first set of growing rows.

Choosing the Size of the Garden

Now that we know where to plant, you need to determine how small or big your garden should be. The size of a garden depends greatly upon two factors: the amount of food you want to grow and the space you have available to grow it.

The good news is that the Raised Row Garden system is perfect for either situation. Whether growing large quantities of food to feed an entire family or just a few basic vegetables, the Raised Row Garden can work with a single growing row, or 50 or more.

Each growing row zone should be 18 inches (46 cm) wide, and the walking zones between each growing row will require between 24 to 30 inches (61 to 76 cm) of space. The length of each row will depend on how much space you have designated for your garden.

You can create a single raised row that is 18 inches (46 cm) wide at any length without any walking row space needed. A great example of this would be in a city or urban setting against a fence, or down the center of a yard. If you do create multiple rows, however, you will need to leave at least 24 to 30 inches (61 to 76 cm) between rows to allow for plant growth, and for space to water, maintain and harvest.

Will You Be Fencing Your Garden?

One final consideration before building your Raised Row Garden is fencing. If you live in an area that is prone to visits from rabbits, deer, raccoons or other invading vermin, a fence can be a great way to eliminate or reduce them. We will cover this in more depth in Chapter 6, but be aware that if you plan to utilize any type of fencing, you will need to accommodate for that space.

CREATING A RAISED ROW GARDEN

Once you have chosen the ideal location and size of your Raised Row Garden, it's time to start building!

Your Raised Row Garden will consist of three main areas: walking zones, growing row zones and planting zones.

A cut-away showing the structure of a first year growing row in a Raised Row Garden. A base layer of organic materials such as straw, leaves or compost is covered with a slightly tapered mound of soil. A heavy layer of mulch is used on either side of the growing rows to eliminate weeding, while providing easy access for maintenance.

Walking Zones

Walking zones consist of all areas of the Raised Row Garden where walking is permitted. This includes the entire area between growing rows, as well as the outer perimeter of the garden. This space is the non-productive portion of the garden, where the soil will never be worked, and plants will never be grown. The walking zones are covered in a thick layer of mulch to eliminate the time, expense and hassle of maintaining them.

Growing Row Zones

Growing row zones are the raised rows with tapered edges where all seed, transplant and root crops are grown. These rows are never to be walked on to keep soil from becoming compacted. They are created with organic materials and covered in some form of mulch year-round.

Planting Zones

Individual planting zones are the immediate area where specific plants are placed within the growing row zones. This area receives direct, focused attention, and the lion's share of the valuable resources (compost, organic fertilizers, water, etc.) that will be used to power your plants. By using these powerful, valuable and finite resources only where they are needed most, you maximize their efficiency.

How you create the three zones above in your first Raised Row Garden will depend on whether you are using existing garden space or starting a garden from an entirely new space. Let's take a look at how to set up either.

BUILDING A RAISED ROW GARDEN FROM SCRATCH

When starting from square one, always begin by clearing the space. Mark off the area and, if grass is present, mow it as close to the ground as possible.

If there is workable soil in the area designated for your new garden space, and you want to utilize it to build your raised rows, this is one time that utilizing a rototiller to break up the soil to create your rows makes sense. Beyond that, you will never need, or use, a rototiller again. Long term, they simply cause too many issues.

There are a few indicators to determine if your current soil is healthy, workable and usable for a new garden.

First, take a standard garden shovel and attempt to dig down 6 to 8 inches (15 to 20 cm) with a single push. Your shovel should sink into the ground with moderate effort, indicating soil that is not too hard or too sandy. Good soil with a healthy structure will crumble apart softly and easily when lifted from below.

Another indicator of good soil is the presence of earthworms. Worms love to work soil that is loose, friable and ideal for gardening. If they are present, it is a good sign your soil is fertile.

If the soil present in your future garden is simply not ideal for growing, you can instead build your raised rows right on top of the current ground space.

Clockwise from left to right: straw, compost, shredded leaves and shredded bark. Just a few of the organic materials that can be used for mulching.

What You Need to Build Your Raised Rows

In order to build your inaugural Raised Row Garden, you will need to use organic materials as a base in your growing rows. Straw, shredded leaves, grass clippings or a mix of soil and compost are used for this process. One word of caution: Do not use hay! Hay contains a plethora of weed seeds that will sprout in your garden all summer long.

If you did not till the ground to use available soil, or don't have access to existing soil, you will need to purchase pulverized topsoil to build your beds.

Mark the Location of Each Growing Row and Walking Row

Begin by marking each of the zones of your garden, remembering that each growing row needs to be 18 inches (46 cm) wide, while each walking row will be between 24 to 30 inches (61 to 76 cm). Walking rows include the space between growing rows and around the perimeter of your garden. If your garden is against a fence or a structure, be sure to leave a walking row on the perimeter of your outside rows as well so you can work those rows easily.

The minimum space needed between the growing rows to allow for plants to expand and grow and for the gardener to maintain the crops is 24 inches (61 cm).

This space also allows proper air circulation and sunlight to find its way to plants. If you have the overall space available, use the full 30 inches (76 cm) for the walking rows, especially between large growing plants such as heirloom tomatoes or sweet corn. It also allows for a little extra growing room for vining plants such as cucumbers, pumpkins and squash. However, avoid making your walking rows larger than 30 inches (76 cm) as this only adds to the cost and labor of maintaining unnecessary and unusable space in your garden area.

Using a tape measure, mark the location of each growing and walking row in the garden space. You can mark your designated areas with whatever resource you have available, such as string, sticks or rocks.

Start at one end of your garden and measure your first row so it is at least 24 inches (61 cm) in width. Mark this area off as your first walking row. Directly adjacent to that row, mark off an 18-inch (46-cm) width area for your first growing row. Repeat this process until you have the required number of rows to match your garden plan.

Keep in mind that you will want a full walking area around the perimeter of your garden.

Step 1-A

Step 1-B

Step 2

Step 3

Creating a Raised Row Garden Growing Row

With your walking and growing rows marked off, you will now build your growing rows. These are the rows that will hold your seeds and plants and will never be walked on.

Step 1. Begin by laying down a 6-inch (15-cm) thick layer of organic material (see "What You Need to Build Your Raised Rows" on page 30) in the center 10-inch (25-cm) area of each marked-off growing row. It is important to loosen compacted straw, shredded leaves and the soil and compost mixture. This allows for adequate water drainage, air and for root growth to expand under the surface during the first year of the garden, promoting optimal plant growth and productivity.

Step 2. Place the purchased pulverized topsoil mix or existing garden soil on top of the layer of organic material. If you decided to till your garden, use the soil that is currently in the areas designated as your walking rows. Simply rake this loose soil up over the layer of organic material.

Step 3. Add soil over the mound of each growing row, tapering the soil across the entire 18-inch (46-cm) wide growing row. It should not have a steep slope, but a flat, middle surface with a gentle taper to the edges. The addition of the soil will compress your 6-inch (15-cm) layer of organic material. Add enough soil so that the center of each completed row remains at a 6-inch (15-cm) height.

Repeat this process to build each of your marked growing rows.

Creating Your Walking Rows

To create your initial walking rows, cover each row in a 4-inch (10-cm) thick layer of organic material. There are a variety of materials that you can use to create your walking rows, and this will be discussed in depth in Chapter 5.

CONVERTING AN EXISTING GARDEN INTO A RAISED ROW GARDEN

If you are planning to convert your traditional or raised bed garden into a Raised Row Garden, you will basically follow the earlier steps as instructed, with a little tweaking. You can choose to till your garden soil for the very last time and utilize the walking row soil available to help create your growing rows. Or, you can ditch the rototiller idea and place your Raised Row Garden directly on top of your existing garden space, utilizing purchased, pulverized topsoil.

WHEN IS THE BEST TIME TO CREATE YOUR RAISED ROW GARDEN?

A Raised Row Garden can be created any time soil is workable—from mid-spring and all through the summer and fall. However, we feel that fall is the optimum time for starting if the timing works out. Creating the space in fall allows a new Raised Row Garden the opportunity to have an over-wintering cover crop planted, which will help build the soil's strength and protect against weeds.

There is also an abundance of organic material available in late fall that's perfect for helping to build growing rows, mulching walking rows and creating compost piles, most notably leaves. One final advantage for creating in the fall—it allows your planting rows to be ready for early spring planting of cool-weather crops. If fall is not an option, spring and early summer are good second and third choices!

THE IMPORTANCE OF PLANNING BEFORE PLANTING

With your Raised Row Garden set up and ready to go, the fun is just about to begin. But before those first seeds and plants go in the ground, there are several things to consider, like what you want to grow, how much space you have available to grow it, where it can best be planted, and when and how it needs to go in the ground.

Your first spring Raised Row Garden will set the stage for the entire year, as well as for years to come.

When it comes to growing a wildly successful Raised Row Garden, the what, where and how much to plant are as equally important as the when and how. With that in mind, let's start first with figuring out the what and how much.

CHOOSING THE RIGHT PLANTS AND PLANT MIX

Before you know where to plant, you need to know what you will be planting. For these choices, it's as easy as following one simple rule: Grow what you, your family and those you will be feeding with the harvest love to eat.

It sounds like such trivial advice, but many gardeners make the crucial mistake of attempting to cram every fruit and vegetable known to the world into their garden plan, whether they like them or not! By mid-summer, it usually leads to a tangled mass of foliage and rotting produce that no one likes or wants to eat. It also leads to one completely frustrated gardener.

Make your Raised Row Garden space count. It's vital to align the plants you want with the space you have available to grow.

Start by creating a list of the fresh produce you and your family love to eat regularly. Be sure to consider not just what you like to eat fresh, but what you want to can or preserve as well. For example, if homemade salsa or pasta sauce is in your future, then make sure that tomatoes, peppers, onions and garlic are on your growing list.

As you make your list, it's also important to keep it centered on the foods that can be grown well in your area. For instance, you may love peanuts, but if you live in Maine, Michigan or the upper Midwest, the growing season is simply not long enough to make it work.

Stick to what grows best in your neck of the woods to maximize your garden harvest. Get in the habit of checking the back of seed packets and plant labels to make sure what you plant will grow well in your garden. Another great resource is your local, county or state extension office. They can be a wealth of information when it comes to what grows best in your area.

Once you have completed your list of what you would like to plant and what will grow well, the next task is to match that list of plants with the space you have available in your Raised Row Garden.

One of the great benefits of Raised Row Gardening is that you can plant heavily in your rows since the soil is extremely fertile. In a Raised Row Garden, traditional spacing requirements can be thrown out the window. Due to the unique design of the raised growing rows, you can decrease most of the standard planting spaces, allowing you to maximize the amount of plants that can be grown per row.

For instance, when planting beans in a row in a traditional garden, most guidelines tell you to space seeds 3 to 4 inches (7 to 10 cm) apart, and allow 18 to 36 inches (46 to 92 cm) between each row. But with raised rows, you can actually plant two planting furrows in a single 18-inch (46-cm) wide row with seeds spaced 2 inches (5 cm) apart.

This allows for a much bigger harvest in a smaller area—a HUGE benefit of the Raised Row Garden system. The same advantages apply to crops like tomatoes, garlic, peppers and nearly all vegetables.

This final task of determining plant spacing will help you determine just how much and how many of your favorite vegetable plants you can grow in your Raised Row Garden.

PARING DOWN THE GROW LIST

If you determine that your list of plants is too long to accommodate the space you have available, then it's time to make some tough decisions. Do you really want to plant that extra row of cabbage, or is it more important to grow the sweet potatoes that you've always wanted to try?

Over the next few pages, we have included three basic garden plan layouts that showcase many of the most well known and commonly grown vegetable plants. Each plan shows the amount of plants we recommend growing in each row, so you can get a quick sense of the potential yields and the variety that you can get with different sized gardens. At the end of Chapter 4, you will find our Raised Row Garden Crop Planting Guide (page 60), taking you through planting instructions for each variety.

Together, these will serve as a great resource as you plan your first Raised Row Garden.

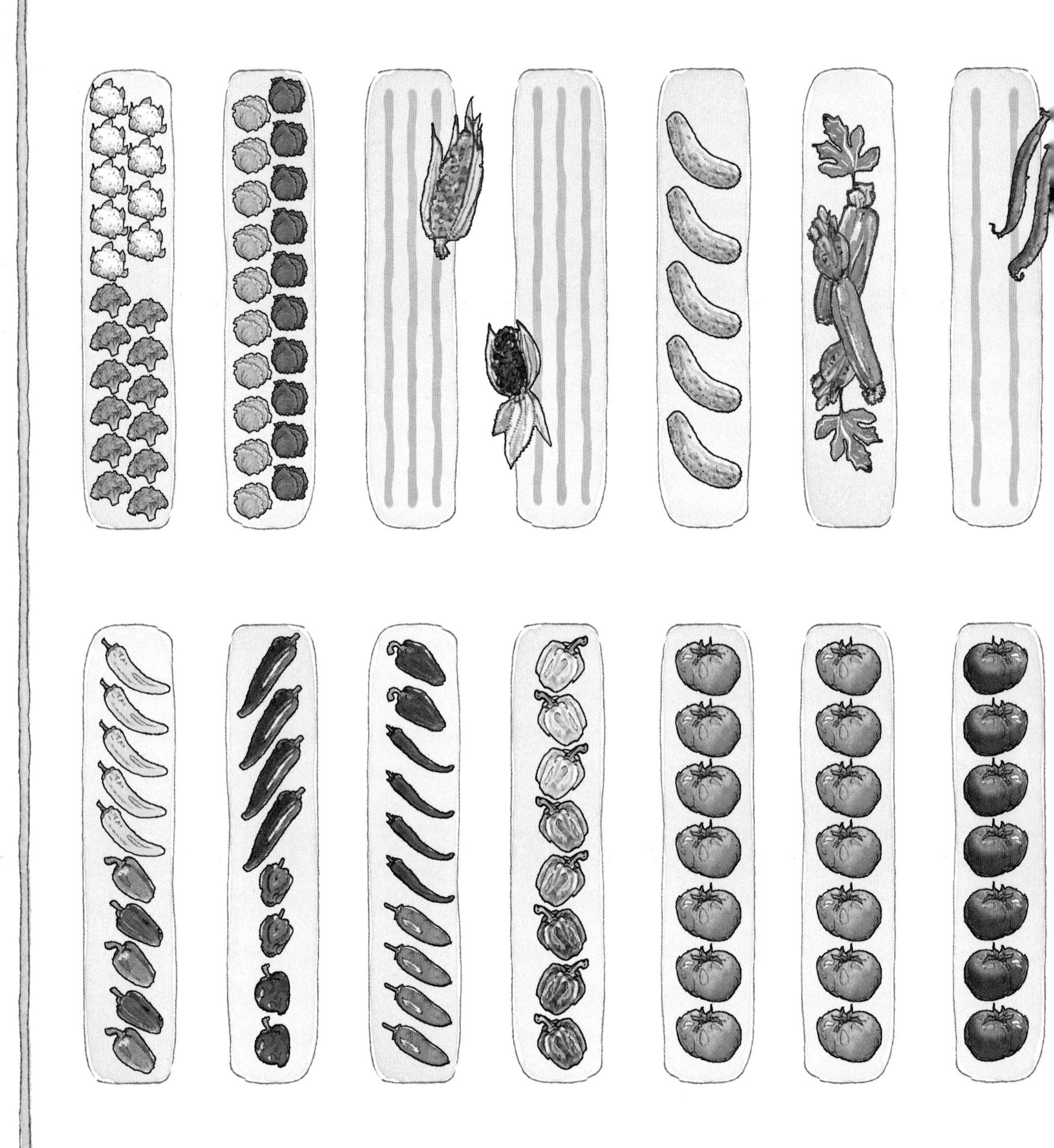

60 x 45-Foot (18 x 13-Meter) Cook's Garden

Space all pepper plants 12 to 18 inches (30 to 46 cm) apart. Space paste tomatoes 24 inches (61 cm) apart and heirloom and cherry tomato plants 36 inches (91 cm) apart. Lettuce, kale, arugula and spinach should be seeded every few weeks to ensure a fresh continuous supply. Reference the grow guide on pages 60 to 69 for the spacing requirements of broccoli, cabbage, cauliflower, cucumbers, green beans and sugar snap peas. Plant corn and carrots in three furrow strips spaced evenly apart down the length of your raised row. Zucchini plants should be planted 30 to 36 inches (76 to 91 cm) apart down the center of your row.

- Cauliflower
- Broccoli
- Red Cabbage
- Green Cabbage
- Ladyfinger Popcorn Corn
- Strawberry Popcorn Corn
- Cucumbers
- Zucchini
- Purple Green Beans
- Bush Lake Green Beans
- Sweet Onions
- Red Onions
- Arugula
- Kale
- Spinach
- Lettuce
- Banana Peppers
- Lunchbox Peppers
- Italian Roaster Peppers
- Heirloom Peppers
- Caj Bell Peppers
- Cayenne Peppers
- Jalapeño Peppers
- Sweet Bell Peppers
- Heirloom Tomatoes
- Heirloom Tomatoes
- Amish Paste Tomatoes
- Sugar Snap Peas
- Carrots

10 x 15-Foot (3 x 4.5-Meter) Salsa Garden

10 x 15-Foot (3 x 4.5-Meter) Salad Garden

10 x 15-Foot (3 x 4.5-Meter) Salsa Garden

Space all pepper plants 12 to 18 inches (30 to 45 cm) apart. Space paste tomato plants at 24 inches (60 cm) apart. Cilantro should be seeded in furrows every few weeks to ensure a continuous fresh supply.

10 x 15-Foot (3 x 4.5-Meter) Salad Garden

Space all pepper plants 12 to 18 inches (30 to 45 cm) apart. Space heirloom and cherry tomato plants at 36 inches (91 cm) apart. Radishes, lettuce, kale and spinach should be seeded every few weeks to ensure a continuous fresh supply.

Once you know what you will be growing, it's time to move on to the critical phase of determining where to place the selected plants in your Raised Row Garden.

MAKING THE MOST OF YOUR RAISED ROW GARDEN SPACE

Where you grow certain vegetables makes a huge difference in the vitality and productivity of your overall garden.

Perennial Crops

The first thing to consider is whether you will be planting perennial crops as part of your Raised Row Garden plan. Perennial crops such as strawberries, asparagus and rhubarb can be excellent additions to your homegrown plant list. Not only do they provide large amounts of produce, they also require only one planting to produce a crop that can be harvested annually for five to twenty years.

In a Raised Row Garden, these crops need to have their own dedicated space that will not hinder placement and constant rotation of your annual vegetables.

It is best to create space for perennial raised rows along one side, or along the outer perimeter of the garden. The rows for perennials can be set up in the identical fashion as annual fruits and vegetables, but confining them to a perimeter area aids greatly in keeping your annual vegetables on a simple rotation.

Companion Planting–What You Grow Where Matters!

In addition to considering important factors like available sunlight and drainage covered in the previous chapter, you must also be aware when planning and planting your garden that some plants perform much better when located near certain varieties, while those same plants will struggle near others. This process, known as companion planting, encompasses the relationships plants have with one another when grown in close proximity. It's extremely important when it comes to the success of your Raised Row Garden.

The concept of companion planting has been around for centuries. One of the more well known of these is commonly called "The Three Sisters." Three Sisters is the practice of planting corn, beans and squash together, and it is said to have been developed, or at least passed down from, the Iroquois Indian Tribe. Here is how it works: The roots of beans help to fix nitrogen levels in the soil. Corn thrives in soil that has large amounts of nitrogen. When you plant the corn and beans together, the corn benefits from the nitrogen. The beans, meanwhile, use the corn as a natural trellis system to grow up. As an added benefit, the bean vines provide extra strength to the corn stalks to help keep them upright from damaging winds.

So what about the third sister, the squash? When planted around the corn and beans, the squash creates live mulch on the soil, helping to conserve moisture and suppress weeds. Squash also makes it difficult for pesky animals such as raccoons to get the corn. Three Sisters is the perfect showcase of companion planting at its best!

The practice carries over and serves well in the Raised Row Garden. For example, tomato and pepper plants should be spaced at least a few rows apart from any potato planting. Tomatoes and peppers are both members of the Nightshade family, and when planted near potatoes, can make them more susceptible to potato blight. In turn, the potatoes can create blight issues for the tomatoes. Knowing these simple companion planting tips can make a huge difference in keeping disease and blight at bay.

In our Raised Row Garden Crop Planting Guide at the end of the Chapter 4 (page 60), we have included companion planting dos and don'ts for each variety. As you plan your Raised Row Garden, use the guide as a reference to help determine what works best for what you will be growing.

CREATING YOUR MASTER GARDEN PLAN

Once you know what can go where, you can start to plan your garden accordingly. Whatever you do, be sure to commit this to paper. Not only will it help you in season to figure out what is growing where (and believe us, you will lose track!), it will be crucial in helping you to develop a long-term Master Garden Plan.

Your long-term plan takes into consideration what crops have been grown where, and where those crops need to be rotated and grown in subsequent years. To make crop rotation easier in the coming years, plan your first year's garden so that similar types of plants are grown near each other. That way, all you have to do is rotate the groups of rows, rather than each single row.

Crops tend to fall in four basic categories: leafy cops, fruiting crops, root crops and legumes. Leafy crops consist of lettuce, spinach, herbs, cabbage and broccoli. Fruiting crops include tomatoes, squash, cucumbers and peppers. Those crops that are harvested in the ground make up the root crops, including onions, garlic, turnips, carrots and radishes. And finally, the legumes, such as beans and peas, actually provide nitrogen in the soil as they grow.

We will discuss crop rotation further in Chapter 10, but keep in mind that moving crops to a new growing row each year helps tremendously in keeping your garden healthy and fertile.

CHAPTER 4

PLANTING YOUR FIRST RAISED ROW GARDEN IN SPRING

Finally, it's planting time! In the Raised Row Garden, there are two basic types of planting methods for the various crops: seeds (including bulbs/tubers) and transplants.

Each has its own simple, but unique, planting style for success in the Raised Row Garden. Let's look at each.

PLANTING SEED CROPS IN THE RAISED ROW GARDEN

Cold-hardy vegetable crops are generally the first to be planted in the garden each year. Unlike tomatoes and peppers, crops such as radishes, kale, lettuce and spinach can be planted by seed early in the growing season, a few weeks before the last frost has occurred.

As soon as the soil becomes loose and friable enough to work with a rake, you can begin to plant these hardy seed crop varieties.

Furrow planting is the way to go when it comes to planting seed crops in a Raised Row Garden. In the Raised Row system, a furrow is a simple trench created in long strips within the growing row zones. Not only does it create a neat and organized system for growing vegetables, but also the narrow 18-inch (46-cm) growing rows allow for direct access when watering and weeding. This system of planting will save you many hours of undesired labor throughout the garden season.

Create furrows in straight strips using a hoe, trowel or garden pick. For smaller, more compact crops, such as fresh greens, radishes and carrots, you can easily plant three full strips in each raised row bed.

For plants that need a little more space to grow, such as beans and peas, you will need to plant them in two furrowed strips spaced equally within the row. This will allow these varieties to grow into large, mature plants without fighting for space. At the same time, it provides enough room to install a center aisle trellis system for pole growing varieties when needed.

Refer to the Raised Row Garden Crop Planting Guide on page 60 for detailed instructions for each common plant variety.

Planting the Seeds

Once you have decided on which rows will be utilized for seed crops, and how many furrows you will need in each row, use your tool of choice to make a furrow strip at the correct depth, as recommended on the back of your seed packet. Next, fill each trench halfway with a layer of compost. As you plant your seeds, push them gently into the compost to the bottom of the trench. This layer of compost helps to retain moisture around the seed, as well as provides a boost of nutrients as the seeds begin to sprout and grow.

Small seeds, such as the lettuce being planted above, should be planted in shallow furrows that have been amended with compost. The compost helps keep moisture and nutrients around the emerging seed, improving both germination and growth.

When sowing seed, always err on the side of putting down a little more seed than you think you need. Not all planted seeds will germinate, and planting a bit more helps to ensure that you will have enough plants for a good harvest. A good rule of thumb is to plant 20 percent more seed than you need to sprout. Be sure to space the seeds as evenly as possible within the rows as you plant. Seeds that are bunched up or planted on top of each other will be difficult to thin out later. Cover seeds by gently raking the soil over the top of the furrow, being careful not to disturb the seed placement.

Furrow planting is also the best way to plant bulbs and tubers in the Raised Row Garden. Onion sets, potatoes, sweet potatoes, peanuts and garlic can all be planted using the same furrow process as with seeds. The only difference is that your furrows will need to be deeper to accommodate the larger size of the bulbs and tubers.

Now comes the watering. Water the furrow strips gently, providing enough moisture to get the soil damp, but not overly soaked. This can be accomplished by a variety of methods. You could use a garden hose with a light mist spray, or a watering can that provides a gentle steady shower along the entire strip. Be sure that you water enough to reach the seed zone. You can test by placing your finger into the soil to see if the moisture has reached down to the depth desired. Remember that it only needs to be moist. Too much water can waterlog seeds and cause them not to germinate. You are only testing for light to moderate moisture at the seed level.

Once planted, mulch the top of the growing row zone (the area above the furrow where the seeds were planted) lightly with a 1-inch (2.5-cm) covering of compost, straw or shredded leaves. We will cover mulching all areas of the garden in depth in Chapter 5, but it is important to remember that all soil in a Raised Row Garden will be covered at all times, including immediately after planting any crop.

After mulching, water your seed crop furrows as needed to keep the level of the soil moisture consistent. How often you need to water will vary depending on your location and the amount of rainfall that you receive. A good rule of thumb is to not let the soil dry out completely for more than 24 hours. If you live in an extremely hot environment, you will most likely need to water daily. For more temperate regions, seed crops can be watered every two to three days for adequate germination.

Succession Seed Planting

When it comes to seed crops, succession planting is an excellent way to prevent your crops from maturing all at the same time. Succession planting is the practice of sowing only a portion of seed to have plants mature for a specific time period.

Using this method, seed is planted at timely intervals so that the harvest times will be spread out accordingly. Although you may love lettuce, it may be hard to eat four rows of it in a weeklong period if it all matures at the same time!

For instance, plant one row of radishes down your center furrow, and, two weeks later, plant a second row on an outer edge of the growing zone. Once two more weeks have passed, you can seed a third row as well. This will help you from becoming overloaded with a large harvest all at once. Succession planting is an extremely useful method for quick-growing crops such as lettuce, kale, spinach, arugula and radishes.

TRANSPLANTS IN THE RAISED ROW GARDEN

With the first of your seed crops in the ground, and as the weather begins to warm, it's time for the post-frost transplant crops to go into the Raised Row Garden.

Transplants can either be purchased from a greenhouse or nursery at planting time, or raised from seed in your own home.

How to Grow Transplants from Seed

Contrary to popular thought, growing your own vegetable plants from seed doesn't require expensive equipment, or a lot of space. There is no need for high dollar grow lights with unique light spectrums. Although they have a place for specialized indoor growing situations such as raising tropical plants, vegetable seedlings can grow strong and true with simple fluorescent light bulbs.

We created a simple indoor tabletop stand by hanging two 4-foot (120-cm) long, dual light fluorescent shop fixtures from a 2 by 4 foot (60 by 120 cm) board placed on top of a few blocks of wood on each end. For lights, we used standard 40 watt, T-8 or T-25 cool white bulbs. The inexpensive fixtures and lights can be purchased at local hardware stores for under $20 each, and can be used for five years or more without so much as changing a single bulb. As an added benefit, they cost only pennies a day to run.

Once seeds germinate in their trays, hang the lights down directly above the plants with a simple screw-in eye hook and a few links of ordinary chain, being careful to keep the light bulbs at 1½ inches (4 cm) above the foliage.

This closeness always surprises some, but it keeps the plants from reaching too high for the light, and it results in strong, more compact plants. As the plants grow, continue to raise the lights to stay 1½ inches (4 cm) above the tops of the plants. With just a few lights, you can grow nearly 100 or more vegetable plants.

We keep our makeshift tabletop stand on our dining room table, but it can just as easily be set up on the floor, or in an unused room of the house. Try to select the warmest area possible to help seeds germinate and grow quickly. With this method, placed in a well-heated room, there is absolutely no need for expensive heat mats to help warm the soil.

Starting your own seeds is extremely rewarding, and allows you to experiment with many plant varieties that local nurseries and greenhouses might not carry.

Nearly all vegetable seeds require a minimum of four to six weeks to germinate and grow to a transplantable stage. If you will be growing your own, simply count backward from your anticipated planting day to know when to start your seeds indoors. We actually prefer allowing six to seven weeks for all transplant seeds started indoors. The extra week or two allows time for the plants to get off to a strong start, and leaves extra time to "harden off" your plants outdoors before planting day. We will talk more about hardening off plants in a moment, but first, let's cover planting and caring for seedlings.

Whether you use commercial, organic potting soil or make your own at home, seed starting mix needs to be light, airy and able to absorb water. There are a lot of great mixes on the market that work well, and most will have either peat moss or perlite as one, or both, of the main ingredients. Peat moss is lightweight and is excellent at absorbing water. Many recognize perlite as the white, foam-like substance found in many commercial potted plants. It may look like foam, but it is actually created by superheating volcanic glass. The glass "pops" at high temperature and turns into the snowy white substance. The super lightweight material is excellent not for absorbing water, but for holding large amounts of moisture around its surface area.

If you do choose to mix your own at home, an equal mix of one part compost, one part sand, one part perlite, one part peat moss and one part worm castings will make an incredibly fertile and productive seed starting mix.

When it comes to choosing germination trays and seed starting cubes, there are several choices that work well. Plastic seed cell packs and trays are a readily available option, as are biodegradable peat pots that can be transplanted directly into the soil. For a less expensive option, you can even make your own individual seed cell containers from old newspapers, egg cartons or cardboard paper towel and toilet paper rolls.

Once you fill the trays with your soil of choice, slightly press the seeds into the mix and then lightly mist with a spray bottle to dampen the soil. Cover the trays with a plastic top and sit them under the tabletop seed stand with the lights off.

There is no need for light at this point, and, in fact, seeds will often sprout better when left out of direct light. It keeps them from drying out, allowing them to germinate faster. Check on your plants every few days, misting the surface of the soil to keep the surface damp. In most cases, you will need to mist every four or five days.

Once a few seedlings have sprouted, remove the lid and place the tray directly under the shop lights, 1½ inches (4 cm) from the top of the seedlings' foliage. Keep adjusting the height as plants grow, being careful to keep them within that close range. This prevents seedlings from becoming spindly and weak.

As you head into the final weeks before transplanting, it's time to get plants ready to go outdoors by hardening them off!

Hardening off is the process of letting young seedlings get acclimated to the fluctuating temperatures, sunlight and airy breezes of the great outdoors.

A few weeks before planting in your Raised Row Garden, and as the weather allows, set transplant seedlings outside in a semi-shady area (screened-in porches are an excellent choice). Temperatures need to be 50°F (10°C) or warmer to begin setting them out to harden off. Start by placing plants outdoors during afternoon hours when temperatures are usually at their warmest. For the first five to seven days, bring your plants indoors in the early evening. After a week, only bring the plants indoors when temperatures fall too low at night, below 45°F (7°C), or if windy and stormy conditions are in the forecast.

When growing your own seedlings, hardening off is an important and often overlooked step. Transplants are under a lot of stress during their first few days in the ground, and getting them used to the outdoor breezes and temperatures in advance helps to keep that stress under control.

How to Pick Out Vegetable Transplants at a Nursery

If space or time is an issue, you can of course always head to your local nursery or greenhouse at planting time to select your transplants. When purchasing nursery transplants, look for strong, more compact plants that have good leaf structure. Avoid the tall, skinny, "leggy" plants, or larger plants that have already started to fruit. The leggy plants will have a tough time standing up to the outdoor elements when planted, while the more mature plants can take much longer to become re-established. Large plants suffer more easily from the shock of transplanting.

How to Plant Transplants

When it comes to transplanting tender, young vegetable plants, start by providing the perfect planting hole with proper spacing.

Although this is the time that most gardeners reach for their shovel, for the Raised Row gardener, it is the post hole digger that will become your best friend.

A post hole digger is the perfect planting tool for the Raised Row Garden. It's as simple as dropping the blade, closing the handles and then lifting out the soil below. In one complete step, you can remove enough dirt to leave a 6-inch wide by 8-inch deep (15-cm wide by 20-cm deep) planting hole. It's also incredibly easy on the back, saving you from bending over to create each individual hole.

Step 1

Step 2

Step 3

Step 4

With the first year setup, it's important to be sure to dig your hole deep enough to break through the ground below the straw or shredded leaves that makes up the bottom layer of the growing row. This is critical in allowing your new transplants to develop and spread into the soil below.

Step 1: Use the post hole digger to create a hole in the growing row. The spacing of your planting holes will be determined by the type and variety of plants you will be using. If you are growing larger variety tomatoes that mature to be 4 feet (120 cm) wide and 6 to 8 feet (2 to 2.5 meters) high, then you need to space accordingly in each row. On the other hand, more compact plants such as jalapeños or bush style tomatoes such as paste tomatoes can be planted at 2 to 3 feet (61 to 90 cm) apart. Refer to the Planting Guide on page 60 for detailed planting and spacing instructions to help you determine proper spacing for transplants.

Step 2: The wide hole left behind from a post hole digger allows plenty of room to add in helpful materials to your fledgling plants. Start by adding ½ cup (64 grams) of compost to the bottom of each planting hole. Remove the plant from the container and lightly spread apart the tangled root base that has formed around the soil block of each plant.

Step 3: Next, set the plant in the hole, making sure the base of the plant is 1 to 2 inches (2.5 to 5 cm) below the soil line. You may need to add some of the soil back into the hole prior to planting, depending on the size of your transplants. With the plant in the hole, water the root base until it becomes soggy to the touch. A good rule of thumb is about 1 cup (240 ml) of water per plant.

Amending your planting hole with organic materials such as crushed egg shells, compost, coffee grounds or worm castings provides young transplants an early boost of nutrients.

Step 4: Fill in the remainder of the hole with garden soil and compost. For every handful of soil that you place back in the hole, add an equal handful of compost. It is also recommended that you add a few crushed eggshells and 1 to 2 tablespoons (4 to 8 grams) of used coffee grounds directly into the planting hole. The crushed eggshells are an excellent source of calcium for plants like tomatoes and peppers, and help to stave off blossom end rot. The coffee grounds, on the other hand, will provide a small boost of nitrogen. You see, a good breakfast is important to start everyone's day off—even your vegetable plants!

Finish off by mulching with a 2-inch (5-cm) thick layer of compost spread 1 foot (30 cm) around each plant.

If you do not have enough compost on hand, you can certainly use shredded leaves or straw as an alternative mulch. Whatever you do, be sure to mulch! Not only will it suppress competing weeds, but also it will help to insulate the root zone of tender young plants from the temperature swings of early spring.

OPTIONAL ROW COVERS

Row covers can be used over the top of your growing rows to protect seedlings and transplants against frost in the early spring and late fall. They are also effective in reducing various insects that may attack your plants and can reduce the intensity of direct sunlight in hot climates during the growing season.

You can drape garden fabric right over your plants or use hoops or a wooden frame to support the fabric above the entire growing row. If you are placing the fabric directly on top of the plants, be sure to loosely lay the fabric on top of the growing row, allowing for the plants to expand and grow. Secure the ends of the fabric with soil, rocks or earth staples to prevent it from blowing off.

When purchasing row covers it is important to determine which type of cloth is most beneficial for your garden.

Frost protection fabric will transmit about 60 percent of available light through the fabric. It is ideal to use in the early spring and late fall to extend the growing season and to protect fragile plants from the cold, extreme winds and frost damage. This type of fabric will protect plants down to 24°F (-4°C).

General, all-purpose fabric transmits 70 percent of available light to the plants below. It not only helps to keep the cold and wind off of your plants, it will protect the plants from frost damage down to 28°F (-2°C). This type of fabric can be used all season long in cooler climates as it allows rain and water to penetrate through the material while keeping the soil warm and unwanted insects away.

Summer fabric can be used if frost isn't a concern. This fabric allows 85 percent of available light to penetrate through and will keep most unwanted garden pests away from your crops as long as plants are completely covered. This fabric will block most pests such as aphids, beetles and cabbage worms.

Shade covers help protect plants that receive intense sunlight and excessively hot temperatures during the summer months. These covers can extend the life of cool-weather crops by keeping the soil temperature down and by reducing the amount of evaporation. They will also help with germination of late summer crops that are planted for a fall harvest. These covers should be mounted above the plants rather than placed directly on top. This will allow the warm air to circulate around the plants and prevent them from being smothered by the fabric.

When using row covers, careful inspection of your plants is crucial, especially during the peak of the growing season. First of all, many plants require bees or wasps to help pollinate them. The row covers should be rolled up or removed during the day once the plants begin to flower to allow for pollination. Cover them up again in the evening when many insects become the most active.

Also, make sure that the plants' leaves aren't becoming too hot under the fabric. If the plants show signs of leaf wilting, remove the cover during the day.

It is important to remember that no matter what row cover you choose, some pests may have already been established prior to planting or placing your row covers on top of your seedlings. Frequent inspection of your plants should occur to determine if any pests have made their way onto your plants.

When row covers are no longer needed, make sure they are dry and store them inside. Properly used and stored, row covers can last for several years.

WHEN TO PLANT SEEDS AND TRANSPLANTS

Knowing when to plant your vegetables will depend greatly on your location. For gardeners in the U.S., the United States Department of Agriculture has outlined zones where plants will thrive in different locations. More than one zone can be located in a single state, so it is best to determine your specific zone by zip code on websites such as planthardiness.ars.usda.gov. Check the seed packet to see the best time to plant the seeds in your zone. Another great option is to contact your local university extension office for specific recommended planting dates, as they will have the most experience and knowledge about your area's growing conditions.

THE RAISED ROW GARDEN CROP PLANTING GUIDE

The guide below will provide you with information on how to plant the most common garden plants. It will also give you the quantity that a standard 20-foot (6-meter) long row can produce of a single crop. Because you may prefer to plant a variety of crops in a single growing row, we have also included plants that are recommended for planting together, and which ones to avoid planting next to each other.

Vegetables That Are Directly Seeded in the Garden

ARUGULA

Plant arugula seeds in the early spring and again in late summer for a second crop. Plant three furrows in each growing row, one down the center of the row and two on either side, placed 4 inches (10 cm) away from center. Space your seeds every 4 to 6 inches (10 to 15 cm) apart, ½-inch (1 cm) deep. Arugula will germinate within seven to ten days and is ready to pick when the leaves are at least 2 inches (5 cm) in height for baby arugula and at least 6 inches (15 cm) for a mature harvest. Arugula prefers cool weather and will quickly grow vertically and begin to flower when it becomes too hot. You can pull out the plant once you notice a thick stalk emerging from the center and when the plant begins to bloom. Succession planting every two weeks allows you to increase your overall yield and extends the harvest period. Plant the middle strip first with 40 seeds, two weeks later plant an outer strip with an additional 40 seeds and, finally, two weeks later plant the other outer strip with a final 40 seeds. Companion plant with beans, carrots, cucumbers, lettuce, onion, potatoes and spinach. Avoid planting next to strawberries.

BEANS

You can plant either bush beans, which don't require a support trellis, or you can plant pole beans. Pole beans grow vertically and will require an external support or stake-a-cage (page 97) to grow on. Plant beans after danger of the last frost. Plant two furrows in your raised row, placing the seeds 3 inches (7.5 cm) apart, 1 to 1½ inches (2.5 to 4 cm) deep. Bean plants provide nitrogen back into the soil as they mature, making them a gardener's dream for soil rejuvenation. Companion plant with cabbage, carrots, cucumber, corn, peas, potatoes, radishes and strawberries. Avoid planting with garlic, leeks, onions and shallots.

BEETS

Plant beets in cool weather when the soil temperature reaches 50°F (10°C). Plant seeds in four furrows at ½-inch (1-cm) depth, placed 2 inches (5 cm) apart. Thin seedlings to 3 inches (7.5 cm) apart. Harvest at any time. Beets can be succession planted to extend the growing season by planting one single furrow, and then two weeks later planting another furrow. Continue to plant furrows every two weeks until all four furrows have been planted. A second fall crop can be planted ten weeks before the anticipated first fall frost date. Companion plant with chives, garlic, onions, broccoli, Brussels sprouts, cabbage, cauliflower, lettuce, radishes and spinach. Avoid planting with beans and tomatoes.

CARROTS

Plant three furrows of carrot seeds four weeks before the last frost. Plant the seeds thickly ¼-inch (0.5-cm) deep and thin carrots to space every 3 inches (7.5 cm). Companion plant with beans, cabbage, leeks, lettuce, onions, peas, peppers, tomatoes and radishes. Avoid planting with dill.

CHIVES

Chives are hardy perennials and can be planted as soon as the soil can be worked in early spring. Plant seeds ¼-inch (0.5-cm) deep down two furrows of your raised rows. Harvest when chives reach 6 inches (15 cm) in height for best flavor. Mature chive plants will spread quickly and will need to be divided by year two or three. Dig up half of the plant and place in another area of your garden or landscape. Companion plant with basil, carrots, marigold, parsley, strawberries and tomatoes. Avoid planting with beans.

CILANTRO

Plant two to three weeks before the last frost down three furrow strips in your growing row. Plant seeds ¼-inch (0.5-cm) deep and place 6 to 8 inches (15 to 20 cm) apart. Crowding cilantro plants is helpful, especially in early spring to keep the roots shaded from the late spring and early summer heat. Cilantro is quick-growing and will bolt and go to seed as soon as the temperatures warm up. You can plant cilantro in the fall as the temperatures begin to cool for a late season crop. Begin to harvest when there are several leaves at the bottom of the plant, being sure to leave a few so that they continue to grow. Once cilantro goes to seed, you can use the seed pod (coriander) as a spice in culinary dishes, or replant for additional cilantro. Companion plant with asparagus, beans, peas, spinach and tomatoes. Avoid planting with fennel.

THE RAISED ROW GARDEN CROP PLANTING GUIDE (CONTINUED)

CORN

For both sweet corn and popcorn, plant after the last frost down three furrows of your raised row, placing the seeds at least 1 to 2 inches (2.5 to 5 cm) deep. Plants should be 9 inches (23 cm) apart. A 20-foot (6-meter) raised row can hold 72 stalks of corn. Companion plant with beans, cucumbers, peas and squash. Avoid planting with tomatoes.

CUCUMBERS

In a traditional tilled garden, you would establish mounds of soil to plant your cucumbers in. In the Raised Row Garden you have already created those mounds by building each raised row. In a 20-foot (6-meter) bed, you will be planting in five areas, spaced 30 to 36 inches (76 to 91 cm) apart. Place three seeds 2 inches (5 cm) apart in a triangular pattern, 1 to 2 inches (2.5 to 5 cm) deep in each of those five areas. Once the seedlings are established, thin each planting area so that there are only two seedlings. You will have a total of ten seedlings. While the plants begin to grow, you will need to move the vines back into the growing row zone to prevent them from expanding into the walking zones. If preferred, you can also place a trellis over each planting area and train them to grow up the support rather than on the ground. Companion plant with beans, cabbage, corn, peas and radishes. Avoid planting with late potatoes.

DILL

After danger of last frost, plant dill seeds in two furrows of your growing row. Plant seeds ¼-inch (0.5-cm) deep, spacing seeds 1 foot (30 cm) apart down the furrow. Dill will grow between 2 to 3 feet (61 to 90 cm) tall. Harvest frequently and early to prevent the plant from going to seed. Companion plant with cabbage, corn, cucumbers, fennel, lettuce and onions. Avoid planting with cilantro and tomatoes.

EDAMAME

This is a bush bean plant that is picked when the beans are green and plump. Plant after danger of the last frost. Plant two furrows in your raised row, placing the seeds 4 inches (10 cm) apart and placing them in the ground 1 to 1½ inches (2.5 to 4 cm) deep. Companion plant with corn and potatoes. There are no plants to avoid with edamame.

KALE

Plant seeds in the early spring and again in late summer for a second crop. Plant three furrows, spacing your seeds every 4 inches (10 cm) apart, ¼-inch (0.5-cm) deep. Succession planting every two weeks allows you to increase your overall yield and extends the harvest period. Plant the middle strip first with 40 seeds, two weeks later plant an outer strip with an additional 40 seeds and, finally, two weeks later plant the other outer strip with a final 40 seeds. Companion plant with cabbage, dill and potatoes. Avoid planting next to pole beans, strawberries and tomatoes.

LEAF LETTUCE

Plant seeds in early spring at a depth of ½ inch (1 cm) and spaced ½ to 1 inch (1 to 2.5 cm) apart. Succession planting every two weeks allows you to increase your overall yield and extends the harvest period. Lettuce prefers cool weather and may not produce well during a hot summer. Plant an additional crop in late summer for fall harvest. Companion plant with carrots, radishes, strawberries and cucumbers. Avoid planting with broccoli, celery and parsley.

LEEKS

Plant leeks in early spring as soon as the ground can be worked. The holes that you plant the seeds in must be deep to allow the leeks to blanch underground, producing the large white area that they are known for. Dig three furrows down the middle and outside edges of your raised beds that are at least 6 inches (15 cm) deep. Plant seeds 3 to 4 inches (8 to 10 cm) apart, resulting in a yield of over 170 leeks in just one 20-foot (6-meter) long bed. Companion plant with onion, celery and carrots. There are no plants to avoid with leeks.

ONIONS

Planting onions is either done by planting seeds or by planting onion sets. Either way, onions are planted in early spring when the ground can be worked. Plant in three furrows down your raised row. Onion seeds need to be placed in the ground at the depth of ½ inch (1 cm) and onion sets at a depth of 1 to 2 inches (2.5 to 5 cm), both spaced 3 inches (7.5 cm) apart. Onions can be harvested at any time, although if you want large bulbs, it will require harvesting in late summer or early fall. In zones four through eight, onions can be over-wintered by placing them in the ground in the fall for an early June harvest the following year. Companion plant with broccoli, cabbage, carrots, lettuce, peppers and tomatoes. Avoid planting with peas and beans.

THE RAISED ROW GARDEN CROP PLANTING GUIDE (CONTINUED)

PEAS

Prior to planting green peas, put a trellis down the middle of your raised row. Do this by using three large landscaping stakes with chicken wire or metal livestock fencing intertwined between the stakes. Even dwarf pea varieties produce better when supported. Plant peas in the early spring as soon as the ground can be worked. Plant at a depth of ½ inch (1 cm), spaced 1 inch (2.5 cm) apart along two furrows on either side of the trellis. Once the peas begin to grow, train them upward by placing them close to the fence so they can reach and climb up the fence. Companion plant with beans, carrots, corn, cucumbers and radishes. Avoid planting with garlic, leeks, onions and shallots.

POTATOES

Plant potatoes in early spring as soon as the soil can be worked. Potatoes are planted using seed potatoes. Cut seed potatoes so that each piece contains an eye. Let them sit overnight to harden the freshly cut skin. In your raised row, dig two long furrows 4 inches (10 cm) deep, and plant each potato piece 10 inches (25 cm) apart with the eye facing upward. As the plant begins to grow, add a mound of soil and organic material, such as shredded leaves and straw, around the base of each plant, leaving no more than 6 inches (15 cm) of the plant exposed. Continue to mound throughout the growing season for maximum yields. Companion plant with beans, corn, cabbage and eggplant. Avoid planting with cucumbers, pumpkin, squash and tomatoes.

RADISHES

Plant radish seeds directly in the soil in early spring as soon as the ground can be worked. You can plant up to five strips within your raised bed. Succession planting is important so that not all radishes are ready for harvest at once. Succession plant every two weeks, which will allow you to increase your overall yield and extend the harvest over a longer period of time. Plant the middle furrow first with 40 seeds, two weeks later plant two additional furrows, 3 inches (7.5 cm) away from the middle row on either side, with an additional 40 seeds in each. Finally, two weeks later, plant the final two furrows on the outer strips with 40 seeds in each. Radishes like cool weather and will quickly go to seed in the warm summer months. Plant another batch in late summer for a fall crop. Companion plant with beans, carrots, cucumbers, lettuce, tomatoes and spinach. Avoid planting with potatoes.

SAGE

Sage is a perennial and does best when planted from divisions of already established sage plants. Divide a sage plant and plant the divisions down the center of your raised row. Harvest minimally during the first year to allow the plants to become established. Companion plant with beans, cabbage, carrots, peas, rosemary and strawberries. There are no plants to avoid with sage.

SPINACH

Plant spinach seeds in the early spring and in late summer for a second crop. Plant three furrows, spacing your seeds every 4 to 6 inches (10 to 15 cm), ½ inch (1 cm) deep. Spinach prefers cool weather and will quickly grow vertically and begin to flower when it becomes too hot. You can pull out the plant once you notice a thick stalk emerging from the center and when the plant begins to bloom. Succession planting every two weeks allows you to increase your overall yield and extends the harvest period. Plant the middle furrow first with 40 seeds, two weeks later plant an outer furrow with an additional 40 seeds, and, finally, two weeks later plant the other outer furrow with a final 40 seeds. Cut leaves when they reach 2 inches (5 cm) in height or higher as this will encourage new and additional growth. Companion plant with cabbage, lettuce, onions, peas, peppers, radishes, strawberries and tomatoes. There are no plants you must avoid with spinach.

SQUASH

In a traditional tilled garden, you would establish mounds of soil to plant your squash. In the Raised Row Garden, you have already created those mounds by building each raised row. In a 20-foot (6-meter) long bed, you will be planting in five areas spaced 30 to 36 inches (76 to 91 cm) apart. Place three seeds, 2 inches (5 cm) apart, in a triangular pattern 1 to 2 inches (2.5 to 5 cm) deep in each of those five areas. Once the seedlings are established, thin each planting area so that there are only two seedlings. You will have a total of ten seedlings. While the plants begin to grow, you will need to move the vines back into the growing row zone to prevent them from expanding into the walking zones. If preferred, you can also place a trellis over each planting area and train the squash plants to grow up the support rather than on the ground. Companion plant with beans, corn, nasturtiums and peas. Avoid planting with potatoes.

SWISS CHARD

Plant two to three weeks before the last frost date. Place seeds ½-inch (1 cm) deep, 3 inches (7.5 cm) apart down two furrows of your growing row. Harvest when leaves are large enough to eat. Cut often to encourage new growth. Companion plant with beans, broccoli, Brussels sprouts, cabbage, cauliflower, kale and onions. Avoid planting with corn, cucumbers and most herbs.

THE RAISED ROW GARDEN CROP PLANTING GUIDE (CONTINUED)

ZUCCHINI

In a traditional tilled garden, you would establish mounds of soil to plant your zucchini in. In the Raised Row Garden you have already created those mounds by building each raised row. In a 20-foot (6-meter) bed, you will be planting in five areas, spaced 30 to 36 inches (76 to 91 cm) apart. Plant four zucchini seeds per area. Thin the seedlings down to two per area once the seedlings have their first set of true leaves. Harvest zucchini when they reach 8 to 12 inches (20 to 30 cm) in length. Companion plant with beans, corn, garlic, peas, radishes, spinach, dill, oregano, marigolds and nasturtiums. Avoid planting with potatoes.

Vegetables That Do Best as Transplants

BROCCOLI

Plant seedlings in early spring and again in late summer for a second crop. Space broccoli 18 inches (46 cm) apart in a zigzag, off-setting row formation, with a maximum of 24 plants in a 20-foot (6-meter) long raised row. This vegetable prefers cooler weather and should be harvested while the buds are still tightly formed and not yet opened up. Cut the main stalk and leave the plant to continue to produce smaller florets for harvesting later. Help repel the damage caused by cabbage moths and aphids by planting marigolds and nasturtiums on the edges of your broccoli row. Companion plant with cabbage, carrots, dill, mint and onions. Avoid planting with strawberries.

BRUSSELS SPROUTS

Plant seedlings in early spring, as this cool-loving vegetable is a slow-growing plant that prefers to be harvested after the first frost. Space seedlings 18 inches (46 cm) apart in a zigzag formation, with the plants off-setting down the two sides of your raised row for a maximum of 24 plants in a 20-foot (6-meter) long raised row. Sprouts will first form from the bottom of the stalk, and will work their way upward as the harvest season progresses. Harvest when individual sprouts are 1 to 2 inches (2.5 to 5 cm) in diameter, working from the bottom up. The plant will continue to grow sprouts at the top and can be harvested for several weeks. This will most likely be the last plant that you pull out of your garden in the fall. As with broccoli, repel damage caused by cabbage moths and aphids by planting marigolds and nasturtiums throughout your Brussels sprout raised row. Companion plant with cabbage, carrots, dill, mint and onions. Avoid planting with strawberries.

CABBAGE

Plant seedlings four weeks before the last frost for a summer crop and eight weeks before the first frost in the fall for a second crop. Space seedlings 12 inches (30 cm) apart in a zigzag formation, with the plants off-setting down two strips of your raised row bed for a maximum of eighteen cabbage plants in a 20-foot (6-meter) long raised row. Companion plant with broccoli, Brussels sprouts, spinach and tomatoes. Avoid planting with strawberries.

CAULIFLOWER

Plant seedlings four weeks before the last frost for a summer crop and eight weeks before the first frost in the fall for a second crop. Space seedlings 12 inches (30 cm) apart in a zigzag formation, with the plants off-setting down two strips of your raised row bed for a maximum of eighteen plants in a 20-foot (6-meter) long raised row. Cauliflower prefers a cooler climate and will develop tiny button-sized heads if it becomes too hot or stressed. As the cauliflower head develops, you must cover it with its leaves. This will naturally blanch the head of the cauliflower to ensure that it will be white and tender for eating. Companion plant with beans, broccoli, Brussels sprouts, cucumbers, corn and radishes. Avoid planting with peas, tomatoes and strawberries.

EGGPLANT

Plant seedlings after danger of the last frost. Eggplants love warm weather and even the slightest bit of frost will damage the plant. Space the seedlings 18 inches (46 cm) apart in a zigzag formation, with the plants off-setting down the two sides of your raised row. This will allow you to plant a maximum of 24 plants in a 20-foot (6-meter) raised row. Companion plant with green beans, peppers, potatoes and tomatoes. There are no plants that you need to avoid with eggplant.

HEAD LETTUCE

Plant seedlings in early spring as soon as ground can be worked. Space seedlings 12 inches (30 cm) apart in a zigzag formation, with the plants off-setting down two strips of your raised row bed for a maximum of eighteen plants in a 20-foot (6-meter) long raised row. Although lettuce prefers cool weather, new seedlings will need to be covered to prevent damage from a hard frost. Companion plant with carrots, radishes, strawberries and cucumbers. Avoid planting with broccoli, celery and parsley.

THE RAISED ROW GARDEN CROP PLANTING GUIDE (CONTINUED)

PEPPERS

Plant seedlings after the last frost date. Spacing requirements vary depending on the mature size of the pepper plant, however a general rule of thumb is to space peppers 12 to 18 (30 to 46 cm) inches apart down the center of the growing row. On average, place ten small- to medium-sized pepper plants, or eight large pepper plants, per 20-foot (6-meter) raised row. Prior to planting, determine where you will be placing your plants. Place a stake-a-cage support system (page 97) 1 inch (2.5 cm) behind each planting spot. This will allow you to have the support in place prior to planting and will prevent any damage to the roots once planted. Companion plant with onions, spinach and tomatoes. Avoid planting with beans.

STRAWBERRIES

Strawberries are perennials and should be planted in a permanent location in your garden, ideally, in an outside row. Plant in early spring when the soil can be worked. Dig a hole deep enough that the roots can spread out easily. At the bottom of each plant where the roots become the stem, the base will form a small crown.

Mound soil in the center of the hole and place the crown slightly above the earth's surface, burying no more than half of the crown in the dirt. This will prevent the crown from rotting. As runners develop, push them into the ground to encourage further growth. June-bearing strawberries will produce a lot of runners and have a harvest season of two to three weeks. Everbearing strawberries produce all season long and will grow more upright and produce fewer runners. Companion plant with lettuce, spinach, beans, garlic, onions, dill, thyme, sage and marigolds. Avoid planting with cabbage family plants, tomatoes, peppers and potatoes.

SWEET POTATOES

Sweet potatoes are unlike most vegetable plants, as they aren't grown from seed. They are grown from slips made from shoots from mature sweet potato plants. You can buy slips or make your own. To make your own, cut a cleaned sweet potato in half. Place each section in a glass of water with the cut half below the water and the top half above the water. It is best to suspend the potato by placing four toothpicks in the side of the potato that is not in water, and allowing the toothpicks to rest on the top the glass. Once the potato begins to sprout, carefully twist off each sprout and place the bottom stem in a bowl of shallow water so the leaves hang over the rim of the bowl. Roots will begin to develop, and your slips are ready to be planted. Plant sweet potato slips three weeks after the last frost date. Unlike other potatoes, sweet potatoes prefer warm weather and cannot tolerate the cool temperatures in the spring. You can plant two furrows of sweet potatoes in your raised rows. Plant individual slips 8 inches (20 cm) apart, with the plant's roots and half of the leaves and main stem below the soil surface. Sweet potato plants are either a vining or bush variety, so depending on what type of sweet potato you planted, you may need to move the vines back into the growing row zone to prevent them from expanding into the walking zones. Each slip should produce 3 to 4 pounds (1.25 to 1.75 kilograms) of sweet potatoes, depending on the variety planted. In a 20-foot (6-meter) long raised row you can harvest up to 216 pounds (98 kilograms) of sweet potatoes. Companion plant with beets, beans and peas. Avoid planting with squash.

TOMATOES

Plant seedlings after the last frost date. Spacing requirements vary depending on the mature size of the tomato plant, however a general rule of thumb is to space tomatoes 24 to 36 inches (61 to 91 cm) apart. On average place nine small paste tomato plants, or seven large heirloom or cherry tomato plants, per 20-foot (6-meter) raised row. This will allow for adequate air circulation around each plant and helps to prevent diseases from transferring from one plant to another. Prior to planting, determine where you will be placing your plants. Place a stake-a-cage support system (page 97) 1 inch (2.5 cm) behind each planting spot. This will allow you to have the support in place prior to planting and will prevent any damage to the roots once planted. See page 92 for information on pruning tomato plants. Companion plant with beans, carrots, lettuce, onions, peppers, radishes and spinach. Avoid planting with broccoli, cabbage, cauliflower, corn, kale and potatoes.

MULCHING IN THE GARDEN

Although vegetable plants and the resulting produce they provide are the stars of the garden, when it comes to the Raised Row Garden, mulch gets the award for best supporting role. In fact, when it comes to the Raised Row Garden, mulch is so important that it more than deserves its own chapter in this book.

Mulch is the backbone of the Raised Row Garden. Its presence in the walking and growing row zones, as well as each planting zone directly around the vegetables, serves a unique and extremely valuable purpose.

The various forms of mulch used within the Raised Row Garden help moisture remain in the soil, suppress weed growth, prevent soil erosion and provide additional organic matter and soil structure to your garden rows. In a Raised Row Garden, some form of mulch will always cover every square inch of space. It is crucial to understand that by keeping the soil in every single zone covered at all times, you eliminate nearly 80 percent of the workload of a traditional garden.

Mulch is what allows the garden to be extremely productive, while keeping the entire space easily manageable. Without mulch, the Raised Row Garden would lose most of its effectiveness.

The secret to total success in the Raised Row Garden is choosing the correct mulch, at the correct time, for each specific zone of your garden. This can include living mulches, such as cover crops in the wintertime that both protect and enhance soil, or compost, whose active microbes and organisms power your plants, or inert mulches, such as wood shavings, straw or pine bark that work year-round to suppress weeds while insulating the soil.

So now that you understand why mulch is so important, let's take an in-depth look at the three mulch zones of the Raised Row Garden.

THE THREE MULCH ZONES OF THE RAISED ROW GARDEN

The mulch zones will follow the basic three zones of the overall Raised Row Garden: the walking zones, the growing row zones and the planting zones. Although each mulch zone serves a different purpose, all are of equal importance to the overall success and ease of maintenance of your garden. As mentioned before, each zone has its own unique requirement when it comes to the type of mulch that can be used.

Later in the chapter, we will take an in-depth look at each of the myriad types of organic and man-made mulches that can be used effectively in the garden. But let's start at the beginning, and see how each specific zone of mulch works and relates to the overall success of the garden.

Walking Row Zones

The walking row zones of the Raised Row Garden are comprised of the all spaces between the growing rows, including the perimeter space that defines the dimensions of the overall garden.

Traditional flat tilled gardens, raised bed gardens, square foot gardens and yes, even Raised Row Gardens, need to have this space included. After all, you need to be able to get to your plants! But in all of the above-mentioned gardens, this space is completely non-productive.

And because it is non-productive, that space will permanently be layered with inexpensive mulch in a Raised Row Garden.

Think of these areas as the no-grow, no-activity zones. Once constructed, the walking row zones are filled with a thick layer of weed suppressing mulch, which tremendously reduces the amount of time and maintenance for this non-productive space. The "non-productive" part is a big key!

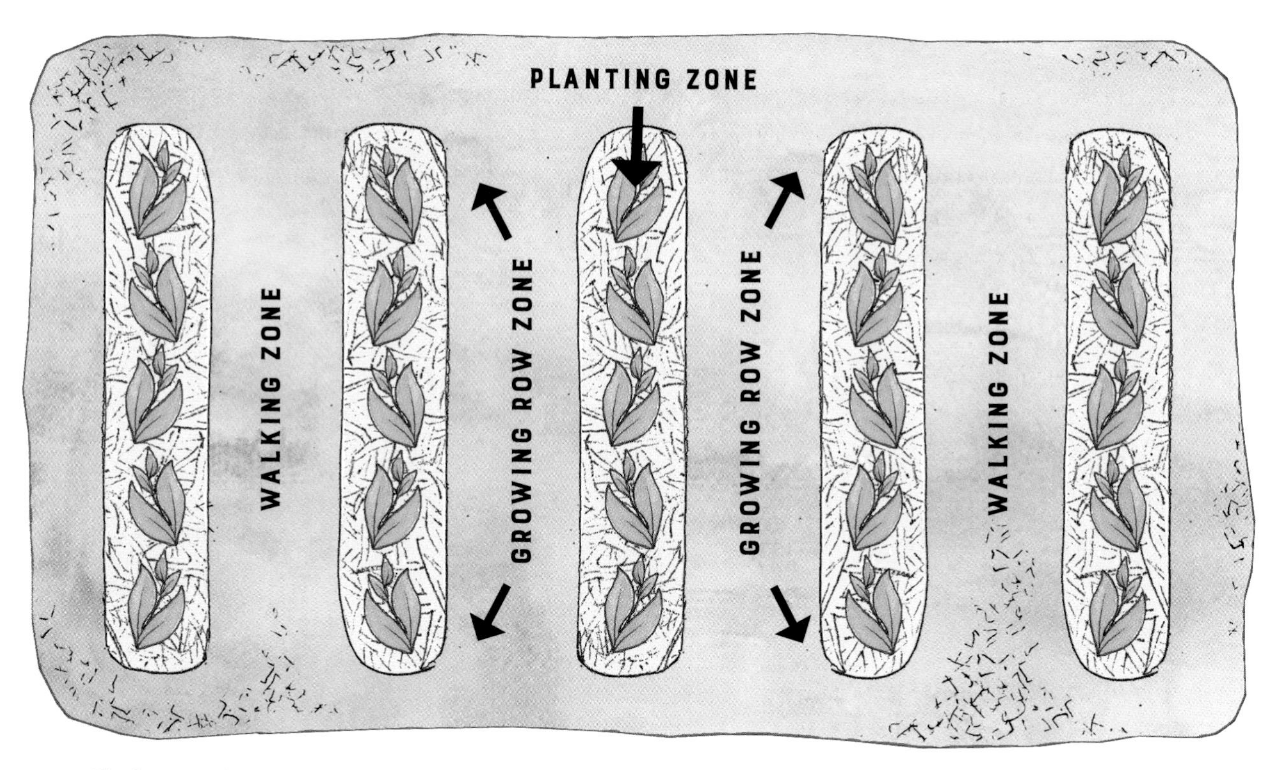

The three zones that comprise a Raised Row Garden: the planting zone, where vegetables are planted and grown; the growing row zone, consisting of the entire area where plants and their roots expand and mature; and the walking zone, the heavily mulched area in between all of the growing zones that allows for easy maintenance without the need for weeding.

Over 80 percent of your overall garden space is dedicated to providing walking areas between and around each growing row. It is crucial not to spend valuable time and resources maintaining areas of the garden that will never be used as part of the growing process.

Because this space will never be used to grow vegetables, it is best to use mulch that is readily and inexpensively available in your area, and one that decomposes slowly. This mulch will never be used to enhance the soil below, and will not affect the soil fertility of your growing rows.

In areas where trees and sawmills dot the landscape, finding by-products, such as shredded bark or wood chips, can be an excellent, cost-saving choice. If you live in area where pine trees are in abundance, use pine needles. Remember that this space will never be used for growing, and the mulch in the zone will never be incorporated into the growing rows.

Mulch levels in this area should be applied to a thickness of 4 to 6 inches (10 to 15 cm) for total weed suppression.

In areas where it is difficult to obtain organic materials, you can improvise by placing a layer of cardboard or newspaper directly on top of the soil. Layer the materials in the walking rows, water it down so it won't blow away and provide a thin, 2- to 3-inch (5- to 7.5-cm) covering of mulch on top of the paper or cardboard for a total of 4 to 6 inches (10 to 15 cm). You will need to monitor the mulch levels in your walking rows each year, adding additional mulch as necessary to ensure you always have 4 to 6 inches (10 to 15 cm) for proper weed suppression.

In addition, do not rake or turn this mulch over, ever! Turning it over plants weed seeds that may have blown in to rest on the surface of the mulch. Disturbing it by raking or turning it over can replant the seeds in your growing rows, causing unnecessary work and resources to be used in the non-productive area of the Raised Row Garden.

At the end of this chapter, we have included a guide to help you through all of the best choices of mulch for each zone (page 78).

Growing Row Zones

Growing row zones are comprised of the individual, 6-inch (15-cm) high, 18-inch (46-cm) wide, raised growing rows. This narrow slice of soil area between the walking rows is the general area where all vegetable crops will be grown each season. The mulch placed in these rows needs to serve a multitude of purposes including weed suppression, soil building, moisture retention, soil insulation and slow-release fertilizer.

A tale of two gardens. On the left in the Raised Row Garden, heavy mulch is utilized to eliminate weeds in the growing row zone. On the right, with no mulch around the plants, weeds easily take over.

Mulch utilized in the growing row zones needs to consist of an organic substance that breaks down easily throughout the course of a single growing season. This allows valuable nutrients to be added and built into the soil, promotes plant health and growth and provides additives to enhance the overall soil structure, which enables it to handle various plantings throughout the year. Just remember, if it doesn't quickly decompose, don't use it in your growing rows!

During the growing season, excellent choices for mulch that can be used in the growing row zones include shredded leaves, grass clippings, straw or a mixture of all three. Although compost can also be used in the growing row zones for mulch, it would require large amounts of this incredibly valuable resource that is best used in the specific planting zone area.

Although wood chips, bark and pine needles are perfectly fine in walking rows, they do not make good choices for mulch in the growing rows. First, they take too long to break down and decompose, and do such a good job of suppressing weeds, that they can hinder the growth cycle of vegetable plants. Second, these substances can change the pH level of your soil, changing it to levels that inhibit vegetable plant growth over time. Finally, they require significant sources of nitrogen to break down; this can deplete the nitrogen levels in your growing row soil, impacting a plant's ability to thrive.

Growing row zones should be covered in a loosely packed 4-inch (10-cm) layer of mulch at all times throughout the growing season. It is important not to overly pack the mulch in the growing rows, such as with unshredded leaves, as they can become matted and prevent water from penetrating into the soil below. When adding mulch throughout the growing season, simply place the new mulch on top of the old mulch. No need to rake the area, as this will encourage weed seeds to enter the soil beneath the growing row zones. Over the winter, the growing row zones should either have a thick cover crop grown within the row, or be covered with a 4-inch (10-cm) layer of packed organic materials such as packed straw or whole leaves. Leaving a growing row exposed with bare soil during any time of the year allows weed seeds to find a new home and valuable soil to be lost through erosion and runoff.

Planting Zone

The planting zone area of the Raised Row Garden is made up of the soil directly around the base of the vegetable plants. For single transplant crops like tomatoes and peppers, and for seed crops that are planted in mounds such as cucumbers and zucchini, this zone is defined as the 12-inch (30-cm) diameter area around each plant. For smaller, seeded crops, or crops grown in long rows such as beans, peas, corn, lettuce, kale, onions, garlic and more, the planting zone area is defined as the portion of soil located 2 inches (5 cm) on either side of the seed row.

The mulch used in the planting zone area is the most specialized and fertile of all, and with good reason. Planting zone mulch must perform like a rock star. It will be used to suppress competing weeds from taking nutrients from your plants, insulate the soil from wild, plant-damaging temperature swings, help retain valuable moisture at the roots where plants need it most and serve as an excellent slow-release fertilizer!

Compost, or a super mixture of compost (page 81), is the single best planting-zone fertilizing mulch. Compost's rich, humus structure is teeming with microbes and nutrients. It works incredibly well in helping to retain soil moisture when used as mulch in the areas directly around plants. At the same time, the nutrients within the compost create the perfect all-natural, slow-release fertilizer.

As plants receive water in the form of rainfall or hand watering, nutrients within the compost mulch slowly seep into the soil, and are then absorbed by the plant's root zone below. These nutrients are taken in as the ultimate slow-release fertilizer throughout the entire gardening season, boosting plant growth and health and increasing the amount and quality of yields. See the chapter on compost (page 115) for information on creating your own compost.

If finding adequate compost is an issue, you can use fresh grass clippings, shredded leaves, dried and aged manure or a mixture of all three as your planting zone mulch.

A word of caution when using manure: Manure, if still too fresh, can easily burn the foliage and stems of plants, even to the point of killing them. Be sure any manure chosen has aged a minimum of six months to a dried, less volatile state. When it comes to the vegetable garden, chicken, rabbit, horse and cow manure are your best choices. Never use household pet manure, such as from a cat or dog. It can easily transmit diseases to your plants.

Apply a 2-inch (5-cm) layer of mulch around the planting zone area for transplant crops. Cover seed planting areas and furrow strips with a thinner, 1-inch (2.5-cm) layer of mulch, 2 inches (5 cm) on either side of where the seeds are planted. This allows seedlings to break through the soil more easily. Once 80 percent of the seedlings have emerged from the ground and started to grow, add an additional 1-inch (2.5-cm) layer of mulch in the planting zone.

By concentrating the use of soil enhancing mulch to only the growing and planting zones in the Raised Row Garden system, you conserve valuable resources. One of the biggest drawbacks of conventional gardening is that compost, or any fertilizer for that matter, is usually spread out over the entire surface area of the garden to be tilled in. That includes 80 percent of the areas that serve as non-productive walking rows.

Raised Row Gardening conserves the most valuable resources to be used exactly where they are needed most–right near the plants!

The first year setup of your garden is critical when it comes to mulch. Don't skimp on the thickness or amounts needed. Rest assured, as each year progresses, you will find yourself needing less and less mulch, and having more and more time to enjoy your garden.

Below is a comprehensive list of both organic and man-made mulches that can be utilized to protect, enrich and power your Raised Row Garden. Along with each mulch type, we have included the zone or zones in which it is best used.

MULCHES IN THE RAISED ROW GARDEN

Organic Mulches

COMPOST

Compost is by far the most valuable and most effective planting zone mulch in the Raised Row Garden. When used within the planting zones, compost releases an amazing amount of nutrients directly into the soil that holds the plant's roots each and every time the garden receives water. Compost is teeming with a plethora of microbial organisms that can power your garden to new levels. Placing a layer of compost mulch in the planting zone will also help keep weeds at bay and will insulate the plant's root zone in case of extreme temperature swings. If you are going to have a successful Raised Row Garden, you need compost! See page 115 for more info on compost.

COVER CROPS

Cover crops are the ultimate living mulch. A cover crop is a live planting of a grain or legume crop designed to protect the soil and give back valuable soil nutrients. Cover crops grow into a thick coat, protecting the growing rows from erosion and weeds. In the Raised Row Garden, cover crops are primarily planted in the fall to protect and feed the soil through the winter. They can also be used in season to protect an unplanted row, or even alongside plants as a living mulch. You can find in-depth information in our cover crop chapter (page 145).

GRASS CLIPPINGS

Grass clippings can come in two forms. Green grass clippings are from fresh cut lawns and are high in available nitrogen. Dried grass clippings are still valuable for weed suppression and as an additive to the soil, but are not a strong source of nitrogen. As an added note, be sure to use only grass clippings from unfertilized lawns in the garden or the compost pile. Many of the additives in commercial lawn fertilizers contain weed killers that can also do damage to your garden and vegetable plants. Grass clippings can be used in all zones of the Raised Row Garden.

HARDWOOD/PINE BARK

The bark from hardwood trees can be stripped off and shredded into large chunks. This is ideal to use in the walking rows of the Raised Row Garden to block seeds from entering through the top layers of the garden and prevent already established seeds from sprouting through the soil up into the walking rows. Although you can purchase bags of hardwood or pine bark, it can also be obtained in bulk at sawmill locations. You can also check with local nurseries and tree trimming companies to see if they have it available for purchase.

MANURE

Aged livestock manure is a valuable planting-zone mulch. When it comes to use in the vegetable garden, chicken, rabbit, horse and cow manure are considered the best source. Never use cat or dog manure, as it can easily transit diseases to your plants and food. Be sure any manure chosen has aged a minimum of six months before use in the garden. Fresh manure can burn the foliage and stems of plants, leading to poor production or even plant death. Although manure can sometimes be found in bags at feed stores, it is most often obtained from local farms, hobby farms or livestock barns for free.

SHREDDED HARDWOOD

When locally sourced, shredded hardwood is most often a blend of various shredded hardwoods. It tends to be more expensive than the by-product of shredded bark and can be found at local nurseries, landscape companies or sawmills. It is extremely effective when used in the walking row zones to suppress weeds.

(continued)

MULCHES IN THE GARDEN (CONTINUED)

PINE SHAVINGS/PINE NEEDLES

Both pine shavings and pine needles contain a high level of acid, but make for an excellent natural source of mulch in the walking zones. In many areas, they are easily obtained and can easily be spread in the walking areas of the garden. Once compacted by normal foot traffic, they both prevent weeds from coming up through the soil, and the intertwining of the pine needles makes it very difficult for weed seeds to enter the garden by penetrating through to the ground below. Pine needles can easily be found in wooded areas, possibly including on your own land. Pine shavings can be purchased at local feed stores, as they are often used for animal bedding, or through sawmills that concentrate on pine wood production.

SHREDDED LEAVES

Shredded leaves are the leaves of choice for use in the growing rows, but also can be used in the walking rows. Shredded leaves maintain the same nutrients that are found in whole leaves, but they also allow both water and air to permeate and percolate into the soil below. Keep in mind that, when using shredded leaves in the growing rows, some varieties are a much better choice than others. Ash, beech, birch, the leaves of all fruit trees and maple leaves are excellent choices. Their pH levels are more consistent, and as the leaves break down, they do not significantly change the soil's pH level. Avoid using large amounts of oak leaves or pine needles, as they both lean to the acidic side and can knock your growing row soil's pH level out of balance. Leaves are easily obtained in the fall and can be shredded using a simple push mower. Leaves that have aged over winter can be crumbled by hand and placed in small areas. You can also obtain leaves from neighbors or landscaping companies who are looking to discard organic materials.

STRAW

Straw, not to be confused with hay, is a farming by-product from a slew of harvested crops. Straw can include, but is not limited to, wheat, rye, barley, oats and other grains. Straw is an excellent choice for mulch that can be easily obtained in many areas. It used to be extremely economical, but the cost has risen significantly in the last few years. Straw is most beneficial when used in the walking and growing row zones. Make sure not to use hay in your garden—hay is filled with weed seeds that will cause you nothing but problems all year long. Straw can be purchased in stores or through local farmers.

SUPER COMPOST MIXTURE

Super Compost consists of a mixture of powerful, organic materials that can power any planting zone. It is the ideal mulch of choice to use immediately around plants in the Raised Row Garden. You can create your own super compost mixture by mixing 1 cup (128 grams) of worm castings, 1 cup (128 grams) of crushed eggshells and 1 cup (128 grams) of used coffee grounds into a 5-gallon (19-liter) bucket of finished compost. This powerful mulch is used specifically in the planting zone to provide the ultimate, slow-release fertilizer and mulch for your plants.

WHOLE LEAVES

Leaves are one of the most naturally abundant and inexpensive mulches. They can be used both whole and shredded in different areas of the garden. Whole leaves are an excellent weed blocker for walking rows, matting together to suppress weeds from breaking through the soil. They also perform brilliantly in keeping blowing and drifting weed seeds from ever finding a home in the garden. Any variety of tree leaves can be used in the walking rows.

Man-Made Mulch

CARDBOARD

When using cardboard as a walking or growing row mulch, there are two things to consider, corrugation and water-resistance. Using corrugated cardboard is much more beneficial than using flat cardboard. Corrugated cardboard breaks down more easily and is easier for the earthworms to consume. This, in turn, results in more castings, which are beneficial to the soil. When determining what type of cardboard to use, be cautious and analyze the original purpose of the cardboard. Some cardboard has been used for long-distance shipping and has been sprayed with a waxy coat that is water and air resistant. If you apply this to your garden, it acts like a plastic cloth, allowing no water or air to soak through to the ground. This type of cardboard takes years to break down and may cause a decrease in the variety of earthworms found in your garden.

(continued)

MULCHES IN THE GARDEN (CONTINUED)

GRAVEL

In areas where it may be difficult to secure large quantities of organic materials, gravel can be an excellent alternative mulch for walking row zones. It is fairly inexpensive, drains well and does a fair job at suppressing weeds. One drawback of using gravel in the walking rows is that weeds can penetrate more easily, leading to more long-term maintenance. If gravel is to be used, it is the one time that using landscape fabric helps immensely. First, cut the landscaping fabric to the dimensions of your walking rows. Lay the fabric on the walking row, securing with landscape u-nails placed on each corner and every 3 feet (1 meter) down the rows. Place a 3-inch (7.5-cm) layer of small size gravel, ½-inch (1-cm) pieces or smaller, over top of the landscape fabric.

LANDSCAPE FABRIC

Landscape fabric can initially be used to cover the walking rows, however we are not big proponents of the use of this material. Although this fabric allows air, water and nutrients to permeate through the fabric to the soil, it does not allow the top layer of mulch to break down. This will eventually become an issue over the years, as weed seeds will tend to spout in the mulch that is placed on top of the landscape fabric.

NEWSPAPER

Newspaper is an inexpensive way to establish starter mulch in the walking and growing rows when you are first getting started. If you already have walking rows full of weeds, just open up a section of the newspaper and place it right on top of the weeds. You will want to place eight to ten single layers of non-glossy newspaper pages over the entire walking row, overlapping the edges so that light and weeds can't peek through. The best way to secure the newspapers from blowing away is to water them with a hose, and then add 2 to 3 inches (5 to 7.5 cm) of additional mulch, such as grass clippings or wood bark mulch, on top of the newspapers to secure them.

When used in the growing row zones, newspaper mulch will not only keep the weeds down, but also it will fertilize the soil, help cool the roots of the plants in the summer heat, add organic material to the soil and save water. Another added benefit is that earthworms will be active underneath the mulch, tilling the ground for you and adding valuable worm castings to the soil.

There has been a long debate on whether newspaper ink and paper is safe to decompose into the growing rows. Most newspaper ink is now soy-based and no longer contains metals and lead, which was found in newspapers years ago. This soy-based product is a natural product and is considered safe as it breaks down into the soil. Also, most newspapers that used chlorine bleach in the past to whiten the paper now use the benign product of hydrogen peroxide, which is also considered safe to humans as it breaks down in the soil. You can contact your local newspaper agency to find out what products they use, but as long as you don't use glossy paper or newspaper with colored ink, it is generally considered safe for use in the garden.

PLASTIC

Although plastic mulch in the growing rows can raise the soil temperature for heat-loving plants such as peppers, tomatoes and melons, most plastic mulches are not water-permeable and are not recommended for use in the growing row zones. Inadequate moisture can stress your plants, lead to blossom-end rot problems on tomatoes and diminish your overall harvest. High soil temperatures can stress your plants and burn up organic matter. In hot climates, most crops will be happier and more productive with soil-cooling mulch such as shredded leaves or straw.

MAINTAINING THE RAISED ROW GARDEN IN SUMMER

WATERING

One of the most critical and time-sensitive chores of maintaining the summer garden is watering. The plants will need help becoming established in the new soil of the Raised Row Garden, as their roots begin to grow and search for the moisture within the soil itself.

Watering needs will, of course, depend on the climate in which you reside. For those living in hot climates with little rain, it will be necessary to water several times a week, if not daily. And for those who live in cooler climates with frequent rain, it may not be necessary to water at all.

Either way, the Raised Row Garden system has a lot of built-in advantages over traditional garden setups when it comes to retaining moisture when needed and repelling excessive water when it's not needed.

When watering plants in the Raised Row Garden, concentrate your efforts directly on the planting zone. This will allow water to come in direct contact with the soil and root zone around each plant and not on the leaves of the plants or in the rest of the growing row zone where roots are unlikely to be located. Not only does this cut down on water evaporation, it also keeps plants much healthier in the long run.

Watering with a full stream or heavy spray directly on plants can injure leaves and stems, and knock off the tender blooms required for vegetable growth. In addition, that harsh spray and subsequent foliage runoff can splash the soil up onto the foliage, making it easier for soil-borne diseases to infect the plants.

Slow and gentle watering of the planting zone is the key. When watering with a garden hose, it is best to take off the spray nozzle, if attached, and use the steady, gentle stream of the water flowing out of the hose in order to water around the base of each plant.

Drip hose rings that deliver water at a slow and steady pace directly to the plant zone are an even better option, if available.

However, if you don't have a hose that will reach your garden and don't have a drip irrigation system installed, you can still provide water directly to your planting zone by using containers of water such as watering cans, or even milk jugs.

Water only the area in the 12-inch (30-cm) circumference that makes up the planting zone of individual plants. Water row seed crops by providing water down the strip where the seeds are planted. It is important to complete watering at a slow and steady pace to prevent the water from splashing up on the leaves as much as possible.

The Best Time to Water

Early morning is the most ideal time to water the garden for both you and your plants. The sun is low in the sky, the temperatures are cooler and the plants are at a low stress level. A gentle watering can give them the drink they need to take on the upcoming heat of the day and more importantly, decrease the risk of water evaporation, leaving your plants searching for water by mid-day.

Midday watering results in less water finding its way to the root zones of your plants due to evaporation. The scorching early afternoon sun can also burn the tender leaves of your plants.

If you are unable to water early in the morning, the best alternative is to water in the late afternoon or early evening. However, you will want to make sure there is enough time in the day to allow the plants to dry before nightfall. Watering in the late evening, where the water remains on the plants until morning, can create a breeding ground for mold and mildew.

How Frequently to Water

Now that you know what time of day to water, another question that most gardeners ask is how frequently watering needs to occur.

Young, tender, just-transplanted plants and just-planted seeds need to have water every day for the first week. The water can come either in the form of rain or water provided by the gardener.

After that, the frequency of watering will be based on your climate, soil quality and plant makeup. If you live in a very hot and dry climate, watering may need to be completed almost daily. However, if you live in an area that is cooler and rains more frequently than not, then you may never need to water again. For those who live in climates somewhere in between, everyday watering can create more problems than it solves.

Plants that get watered every day never send roots deep into the soil to look for soil moisture and nutrients. This creates a weak root system that leads to a weak and feeble plant. Plants that are forced to become more self-reliant establish deeper and healthier roots that can take in and absorb adequate water and nutrients for optimal growth on their own.

The best way to determine whether or not you should water is to get to know your plants. If the edges of your tomato plants leaves begin to curl up, the plant is telling you that it needs water. If your pepper plant that once stood tall and upright has drooping leaves that are pointing towards the ground, then you most likely need to give it a drink. Take note of what your plant looks like, and observe if there are any changes in the leaf and stem appearance during hot spells to detect if your plant is suffering from a lack of water.

If you are unsure if your plants need water, dip your finger ½ inch (1 cm) into the plant zone soil. If you pull your finger out and the ground was dry, then you need to water. If it is still moist, watering is not required.

How Much to Water

One of the major benefits of a Raised Row Garden is that during watering, water is only provided in the planting zone area, which allows moisture to be absorbed directly into the plant's roots. Even better, with the addition of mulch in this zone, the evaporation percentage is minimal.

This Raised Row watering system allows for less water to be used than in a traditional garden. This is due to the fact that the planting zone soil absorbs and retains the moisture right where it is needed, at the plant's roots. There is no reason to water the entire garden, only the planting zones where the roots are located.

This will save you from watering over 80 percent of your garden space by eliminating the need to provide additional water to the growing and walking rows. For instance, a traditional garden that has been watered with a rotary sprinkler will provide 80 percent of the water to non-productive and non-growing soil. Even worse, when watered on a windy day, a sprinkler will lose water rapidly into the environment due to evaporation. On the contrary, a Raised Row Garden that has been watered directly at the planting zone level will utilize significantly less water and will be able to retain the moisture level content at a much higher rate due to the mulch protecting the soil from environmental elements, such as wind.

During the first seven days after transplants have been moved into the garden, provide each transplant ¼ to ½ gallon (1 to 1.75 liters) of water on days when the rain cannot provide that amount. As transplants become acclimated to their new home, you may notice that their growth appears stunted or that their leaves don't look as good as when they were growing in their seedling container. This is not necessarily a signal to provide more water. An adjustment period is normal when transplants are moved away from the familiar soil and protection of a container. The plant now must adjust to not only new soil, but also to harsh swings in environmental conditions when placed in the garden for the first time.

After those initial seven days, water the plants as necessary to keep them healthy.

When you determine that it is time to water, use ¼ to a ½ gallon (1 to 1.75 liters) of water per plant. You may need to adjust the amount depending on the size of the plant and weather conditions. For instance, a large heirloom tomato plant at week six after being planted will require more water than the same plant at week three. There is no need to complete the finger test again to determine if your plants need more water. Simply add more water to larger plants when they begin to look wilted as compared to a smaller plant that appears the same way. If you are using a standard ½-inch (1-cm) garden hose at full strength, it will typically take five seconds to deliver just over ½ gallon (1.75 liters) of water to each planting zone.

PRUNING AND PINCHING PLANTS

Once your plants become established, they will begin to grow at what seems to be a record pace. In no time you will be faced with large plants that are producing branches and leaves in all directions.

Although this may seem like you are on track for growing record-breaking vegetables, too many branches with too many leaves is not always a good thing. If left to grow without any intervention, vegetable plants concentrate their effort and energy on growing green, leafy foliage and limit the number of flowers and vegetables that they produce. This, in turn, will lead to lower yields and smaller-sized produce than desired.

There are two ways to encourage the size and yield of your vegetables and limit useless leafy production on your plants: pinching and pruning. Pinching is the process of using your fingers to remove flower buds, small stems and immature fruit as the plant grows. Pruning requires the use of shears to remove entire branches of your plant or vine.

Both pinching and pruning help keep your garden healthy by eliminating unnecessary foliage, flowers and branches. This not only allows the plant's energy to be focused on producing high-quality yields, but it also improves air flow and circulation between the branches, which improves pollination, disease control, pest control and ripening rate. Another benefit to pinching and pruning is that you can train plants to grow where you need them to, including up trellises, stakes and other garden supports.

Pinching

Pinching can involve several tasks when it comes to one of the most popular garden plants, tomatoes. As tomato plants get bigger, they produce energy and develop additional stems and suckers throughout the growing season. Suckers are new branches that grow out of the tomato's main stem, just above another branch. Suckers that emerge during the growing season are nearly always weak, produce inferior fruit and drain away energy from the main stem.

Using your thumb and index finger pinch off all suckers that grow at the joint between the plant's main stem and leaves during the entire growing season.

Pinching off excessive blooms on flowering plants such as large tomato, cucumber and squash plants will help your remaining fruit grow larger and mature more quickly. Remove one-third of your blossoms as they appear, allowing the energy of the plant to focus on growing sizeable produce rather than a lot of small fruits.

After the fruit has set, pinch away any produce that is too close, deformed, diseased, insect-bitten or that is not getting sufficient light and air circulation. This will eliminate poor growing conditions that drain the plant's energy on healing wounds and ripening bad fruit. Also pinch away any foliage that comes in contact with the actual fruit. By removing the leaves that are touching the produce, you are eliminating a chance for pests and diseases to have direct access to the fruit.

Pruning

There are several reasons why you need to prune plants in the garden. First of all, pruning improves the amount of light and air flow around each individual plant. This will lessen the threat of pests and diseases from entering overcrowded areas. Just like pinching, pruning improves the quality and size of your harvest by cutting off growth that is non-productive, allowing the plant's energy to concentrate on growing high-quality produce.

Another benefit is that you are able to control the size of your plant through pruning. This is crucial for larger-growing plant varieties, such as heirloom tomatoes. These plants can grow larger than 6 feet (1.75 meters) tall, and pruning may be necessary to control the excessive growth so that they don't crowd out other plants in the same or adjacent growing rows. Keeping plant foliage away from other plant foliage is important to prevent the spread of disease from one plant to another.

For plants that you want to train to climb a trellis, such as cucumbers, pruning will help you keep the vine thinned and trained upward.

HOW TO PRUNE TOMATO PLANTS

Of all vegetable plants, the tomato plant requires the most attention in the form of pruning mid-season.

Pruning enhances the production of tomato plants, which results in more tomatoes, bigger tomatoes and even more flavorful tomatoes.

Once the tomato plant reaches 12 to 18 inches (30 to 46 cm) in height, remove the bottom 6 to 8 inches (15 to 20 cm) of branches and foliage at the base of the plant. This will decrease the chance of soil splashing on the leaves that hang closest to the ground.

Additional pruning of branches in the middle and top portion of the plant will be determined by what variety of tomato plant you have planted in the raised row.

Determinate tomatoes, or tomato plants that are bred to be compact and to stop setting fruit once they reach the top bud, set the bulk of their crop over a two- to three-week period. Each plant will produce a limited number of fruits before stopping production. Prune only the branches that appear below the first cluster of flowers. Do not prune branches above the first cluster or those that have flowers on the stem, or you will reduce your overall yield.

Indeterminate tomato varieties, or tomato plants that will continue to grow all season long and typically reach heights of 5 feet (1.5 meters) or higher, will grow and set fruit until they are killed off after the first frost. Pruning branches in the middle and top of the indeterminate tomato plant helps produce an abundance of fruit. As the growing season progresses, continue to prune branches within 1 foot (31 cm) of the soil to decrease the risk of tomato blight.

As all tomato plants mature, their lower leaves begin to yellow. Remove yellowed leaves and branches to prevent disease, improve the tomato plant's appearance and help the plant keep its energy focused on healthy fruit production.

One word of caution about pruning: If you grow tomatoes in an area that is hot with excessive direct sunlight, be careful not to over-prune your tomato plants. Steady and intense sunlight that has direct access to the fruit itself can lead to tomatoes developing sunscald. It may be more beneficial to keep some of the leafy foliage to shade and protect your tomatoes from being damaged by the sun's rays.

In addition to tomatoes, peppers can benefit from low-level pruning to allow light for ripening. Remove the bottom 10 percent of your pepper plant's branches to allow for adequate air circulation and light.

SUPPORTING YOUR PLANTS

Many garden plants will need some extra support in order to reach maximum yield potentials. If you have gardened the traditional way in the past, you will notice that with the improved growing conditions, Raised Row Garden vegetable plants will grow at a faster rate.

You have set your plants up for success by building up the growing rows with organic matter, providing them with healthy and well-drained growing soil and allowing their roots to be undisturbed by developing specific walking rows. Now that you have begun to pinch and prune, it is time to give them a little extra support to make it through the summer.

Even with the use of a trellis, it may be necessary to provide extra support to your vegetable plants by tying up large or heavily fruited vines and branches. Here, an abundant crop of tomatoes is tied to a trellis to keep the plant from toppling over.

It is ideal to install your supports and trellis systems prior to actually planting seeds or transplants. This lessens the chance that you will disturb the roots or plants after they have been planted.

There are various trellis systems, stakes and cages that are available for purchase. However, you can quickly make your own at a much lower cost than purchased ones.

Trellis System

The quickest and easiest trellis system for climbing vines, such as peas, pole beans and cucumbers, is a simple fence post and fence combination. Place two large metal fencing stakes in the ground on each end of the raised row. Add a middle support if your row is greater than 10 feet (3 meters) in length. Tightly secure livestock fencing to your stakes using twist ties or wire and your trellis is complete!

As your vine crops begin to grow, train them up the trellis. They will grab the fence panel and will be supported for the summer.

There are several other ways to support climbing crops. You can use commercially-bought trellises, arbors and arches, or you can even design your own trellis system using materials that you have in your own home or backyard.

Large sticks or sturdy bamboo canes buried in the growing row next to the climbing vines make for an instant and inexpensive support system. Just train young vines to go around or climb up the stick by wrapping them around each support. For larger, heavier vine crops such as cucumbers or melons, a horizontal support stick can be tied with twine or wire to the tops of the sticks or canes for a sturdier support.

For lightweight crops such as sugar peas or pole beans, replace some of the horizontal sticks or canes with twine or rope for an easy and inexpensive trellis system.

You can even make a teepee support by placing six to eight sticks in the ground around a 12-inch (30-cm) circle, with the tops coming together and tied with string, twine or wire. Use lighter sticks for lightweight crops and sturdy sticks for heavier crops such as cucumbers or melons.

You can also make your own ladder trellis by adding sections of rope or thin strips of wood placed 6 inches (15 cm) apart between two larger sticks. Place the trellis upright in your growing row or angle and tie additional rear stick supports at the top of your ladder for a step-ladder look.

Get creative and use whatever you have available to make your own unique trellis support system.

FERTILIZING THE RAISED ROW GARDEN

Fertilizing the Raised Row Garden is simple and easy to do. You will concentrate all of your fertilizing efforts and resources directly in the planting zone. No need to waste valuable fertilizer products in areas where nothing is grown.

Organic fertilizers provide the best nutrients and minerals for a healthy garden because they are naturally occurring. Beyond the obvious benefits of keeping chemical fertilizers out of the garden and off the produce that is consumed, organic fertilizers can actually help to build soil fertility over time. Many synthetic fertilizers are laden with salts that can destroy soil structure. This requires constant amending of the garden soil to achieve a healthy and productive soil structure. Organic fertilizers on the other hand, provide humus and organic matter back into the soil, which improves the quality and balance in the soil structure to grow strong and healthy plants year after year.

There are several organic fertilizer products on the market and many that are available for free. Below are some common fertilizers that are best used in a Raised Row Garden system.

Compost

Finished compost adds beneficial microorganisms, greatly improves soil health and increases earthworm activity in your soil. It is applied as a fertilizer when placed around the base of your plants in the planting zone. This method of fertilization is considered slow release—releasing nutrients into the soil over time with rainfall and watering. Add your first fertilization application of compost as soon as you place transplants in the ground. Place a 2-inch (5-cm) layer of compost in a 12-inch (30-cm) circumference within the planting zone.

STAKE-A-CAGE SUPPORT

Most commercial cages for plants such as tomatoes, cucumbers and peppers, have a hard time supplying the strength needed to support plants, especially when growing large heirloom varieties. And with the widespread growth of the stems, a single stake isn't always your best option, either.

You can make your own support system, which we have termed as the stake-a-cage. It takes the best properties of a support cage and combines them with the sturdiness of a large wooden stake. It can be used on nearly any vegetable plant to provide incredible support.

Wire Cutters

Fencing U-nails

Hammer

Saw (jigsaw, hand saw or chop saw)

2 by 2-inch (5 by 5-cm) wooden stakes, one per plant, cut to desired length. We use 5-foot (1.5-meter) stakes for supporting larger plants, 3- to 4-foot (1- to 1.25-meter) stakes for medium sized plants and 18- to 24-inch (46- to 61-cm) stakes for smaller plants.

1 roll 30-inch (76-cm) high welded-wire galvanized fence with a 2 by 4-inch (5 by 10-cm) mesh grid

---

1. On each stake, make a sharp point so it can easily penetrate the garden soil. Use a jigsaw to make angled cuts on all four sides of one end of your stake. You will want the end of your stakes to resemble a pencil point.

2. Roll out the galvanized welded wire roll, and use wire cutters to snip off 18-inch (46-cm) wide sections for supporting large plants, or 12-inch (30-cm) wide sections for medium to small plants.

3. Place the wire grid on the stakes with the bottom of the wire about 14 inches (35 cm) from the bottom of the stakes. This allows the stake to be driven in to that depth, so for smaller stakes you can use less space. Using a hammer, nail three fencing U-nails, one at the top, one in the middle and one at the bottom of each stake, to secure the wire to the stakes.

4. Place your supports in the ground by hammering them into the growing row 1 inch (2.5 cm) from where the plant will be or is planted.

You will also use compost as a fertilizer for the small seed row crops on the day that the seeds are planted. Add a 1-inch (2.5-cm) layer of compost within 2 inches (5 cm) of either side of the seed-planting strip. Once 80 percent of the plants have emerged and are growing, add an additional 1-inch (2.5-cm) layer of compost.

Compost that is applied in the planting zone doubles as the mulch for this area. It is a win-win for plants.

Compost Tea

Compost tea is a simple mixture of fresh compost steeped in water for five to seven days. Water mixed with compost will absorb many of the beneficial nutrients from the composted materials.

If compost is called black gold, then compost tea must be called liquid black gold. It is the gold standard of organic fertilizing. When applied directly to the plant zone, compost tea will feed your plants directly at the root level. In addition, you can apply it directly to the leaves with a spray bottle in a process known as foliar fertilization. Unlike synthetic fertilizers, compost tea won't add unnecessary salts, which can slowly destroy the balance of your soil structure.

Compost tea can initially be applied to your garden once transplants have been in the ground for two weeks. You can also use compost tea as a fertilizer booster for seed crops three weeks after the plants have emerged from the ground. As with watering, it is best to apply early in the day before the sun is too hot to decrease the chance of the compost tea burning the leaves of plants.

Repeat the fertilizing process as needed every two weeks, for a maximum of four applications.

If you don't make your own compost, you can purchase ready-to-go compost or compost tea bags to make your own compost tea brew at home.

HOW TO MAKE YOUR OWN COMPOST TEA

In order to make compost tea all you need is two 5-gallon (19-liter) buckets, water and compost. There are many strategies to make compost tea. However, we have found this method to be easiest, most effective and, most importantly, the simplest!

2 (5-gallon [19-liter]) buckets

1 (5-gallon [19-liter]) bucket lid

Large stir stick

Water

1.5 gallons (5.75 kilograms) of finished compost

1. Fill a 5-gallon (19-liter) bucket with 1½ gallons (5.75 kilograms) of finished compost. Use the compost from the bottom third of your compost pile.

2. Fill the bucket with water, stopping once the water level reaches 2 inches (5 cm) below the top of the bucket. It is best to use well water that has not been put through a softener, or rainwater whenever possible, as residual traces of salt and/or chlorine is present in treated water. If you only have access to city or softened well water, fill an open container with 4 gallons (15 liters) of tap water and set outside three days prior to making your compost tea. The sun and air will help eliminate the undesirable chemicals.

3. Stir the compost with the long stick, or the end of your garden shovel, at least three times per day, for five to seven days. The subsequent aeration and stirring of the compost helps to release additional nutrients into the water.

4. At the end of five to seven days, strain the mixture through a piece of burlap, a mesh screen or over a large strainer over the second 5-gallon (19-liter) bucket. Store in a cool, dark location until ready to use with an airtight lid for best results.

5. Discard the solid remnants back into your compost bin.

WHEN AND HOW TO APPLY COMPOST TEA

Pour your compost tea into a watering can or a simple garden sprayer. Soak the planting zone soil with the compost tea as if you were using plain water. You can also provide the leaves of each plant with a light spray of the solution. The minerals and nutrients are then absorbed through the leaves, also known as foliar absorption, as well as through the root zone, maximizing fertilization efforts. It is best to apply in early morning or late evening, when the threat of sun scalding is minimal.

Repeat the compost tea application every two weeks for a maximum of four applications. If you continue to fertilize, all the growth effort will be concentrated in the foliage, rather than developing blooms that will grow into fruits and vegetables. The plant will develop strong roots and stems the first six to eight weeks after planting with the help of the natural fertilizer.

Worm Castings

Worm castings, also known as vermicast, are an organic form of fertilizer produced from earthworm waste. Worm castings, when applied as fertilizer, provide vital amounts of organic material, including nitrogen, calcium, magnesium, phosphorus and potassium, into the soil for the vegetable plants to absorb. Not only does it boost the plant's production, but it also improves soil aeration, drainage and water retention in the soil. Another benefit of using worm castings is to repel pests such as aphids and spider mites that are in and around the soil.

To use worm castings as a slow-release, granular fertilizer, directly apply a small handful of the castings around the base of each plant within the plant zone area. Worm castings can initially be applied to your garden once transplants have been in the ground for two weeks. You can also use the castings in the raised rows that hold seed crops three weeks after the plants have emerged from the ground.

Worm castings can also be used to make an all-purpose, liquid fertilizer. Simply mix ½ to ¾ cup (64 to 96 grams) of castings with 1 gallon (3.75 liters) of water, and steep for a minimum of 24 hours. Shake or stir the mixture frequently. Strain the liquid, and place in a spray bottle or garden sprayer. Using the same fertilizing timeline as solid worm casting applications, water the foliage of each plant just until the water begins to run off. Water in early morning or evening to prevent leaves from burning during the heat of the day.

Worm castings can be bought at garden centers, through online vendors or even be made in your own backyard!

To make your own worm castings, take a 12-inch (30-cm) deep rectangular plastic bin with a lid, and drill several holes in the bottom and lower sides of the container. Add 2 inches (5 cm) of organic material such as shredded newspaper, shredded leaves, straw and grass clippings to the bottom of the container. Add a 1-inch (2.5-cm) layer of soil mixed with compost. Moisten and wait 24 hours before adding earthworms to the mixture. You will need 1 pound (454 grams) of red wiggler worms for every square foot of the container.

Add finely chopped fruit and vegetable scraps to the soil mixture, mixing it in the soil to prevent it from spoiling to feed the worms. Feed them once a week for the first few weeks using any organic material that you would typically place in a compost pile. As the population begins to grow, feed them each week, a quart of food scraps for each square foot of the container.

Make sure to keep the lid on the container and keep it in a cool, dark spot. Many people will keep them indoors, under a sink or in the basement, if it is too warm outside. There should be little to no smell from the container.

When you are ready to use the castings, open the container and dump the entire contents on a flat surface. Prepare the bin with the original set up of organic material, soil/compost, moisture and fruits/vegetable scraps. Handpick the worms from the bin and place them back inside the container.

The castings that are left over can be stored in a closed container until ready to be used.

Used Coffee Grounds

Used coffee grounds are an incredibly rich source of nitrogen that can easily be added to your compost bin or used as a fertilizer in your raised rows.

The benefit of using coffee grounds as a fertilizer is that it adds organic matter to the soil, improving aeration, drainage and water retention. When absorbed through the soil, used coffee grounds create an area that beneficial microorganisms and earthworms migrate towards. The grounds also deter slugs and snails from the base of your plants.

When applying coffee grounds directly on your soil as fertilizer, it is important to use brewed coffee grounds rather than fresh. Fresh coffee grounds are high in acid content and can change your soil's pH levels prior to being composted. Used coffee grounds, on the other hand, are safe to use directly in your Raised Row Garden.

Sprinkle a few teaspoons of grounds around each plant once transplants have been in the ground for two weeks. You can sprinkle grounds in the raised rows that hold seed crops three weeks after the plants have emerged from the ground.

DEALING WITH UNWANTED BUGS, CRITTERS AND DISEASE

Because this is your first year with your Raised Row Garden, you won't know what to expect when it comes to what pests and diseases might enter your garden.

The first line of defense in any garden is to have healthy and well-maintained soil. By adding nutrients and organic matter to your growing rows, you have already taken the first step in helping to initially eliminate pests and disease.

However, one of the daunting chores in maintaining a summer garden is to eliminate, or reduce, the damage caused by pests and disease.

Here are some ways you can help eliminate problems during your first full Raised Row Garden season, and beyond.

Stroll through the Garden

The first line of defense against anything is monitoring what is happening in your garden. Make it a daily habit to walk up and down your walking rows and note any changes in your plants from the day before. Early detection of any issue is a huge key in preventing crop and plant loss! In just a few days, an unnoticed tomato hornworm can turn into loss of an entire tomato plant.

If something looks different than it did the day before, then take a closer look. For instance, if you see chewed holes in your cabbage leaves, then you might have cabbage worms living in between and under your leaves. Pull back the large outer leaves and peak inside and under each leaf. If you see any small worms, worm residue or eggs, you know that you will need to take action to prevent further damage.

The Raised Row Garden setup makes this chore simple. Plants are located in defined spaces with the walking rows covered in mulch, making it easy to navigate rows even after heavy rains.

Remove Damaged Leaves, Branches and Produce

If you notice that you have dying or diseased branches or leaves, remove them from your garden and discard them away from the garden area. If there is damage on the produce itself, whether from pests, diseases or animals, remove the produce from your plant immediately. Leaving damaged produce on the vine soaks up the energy of the plant as it tries to heal itself, taking away from younger and healthier fruit. In addition, damaged foliage and fruit will attract more predators to the plant.

Handpick Harmful Bugs and Insects from Your Plants

Once you have identified damage from pests, it is time to act. Handpicking unwanted pests and removing them daily works! On those daily walks, remove harmful pests such as beetles, cabbage worms and tomato hornworms by hand as you see them. If you prefer, you can use garden gloves, tongs or even a garden shovel to remove the bug from the plant. The simple act of removing these larger bugs will keep insect populations under control and manageable during the first Raised Row Garden season. One of the biggest mistakes made by gardeners is to instantly reach for bug sprays. Remember that these sprays kill just as many beneficial insects, and killing them can disrupt the natural harmony of the garden.

Continue to Build Organic Matter into Your Soil

Keep amending your soil with natural organic materials through mulching and apply natural fertilizers to continue to develop strong, vigorous plants. A healthy plant is able to withstand various pests and diseases without much damage. Even if you have a few bites out of a leaf from an unwanted predator, a healthy plant can continue to thrive.

Water in Early Morning

As discussed earlier, it is important to water in the morning before the heat of the day beats down on the plants. Not only will this ensure that the foliage doesn't burn from the sun's rays, but it will also help to decrease insect and fungal damage to your plants. Wet foliage from a late evening watering attracts insects and becomes a breeding ground for mold and mildew.

Disinfect Tools and Gloves

If you've been working with a diseased or infested plant, clean your tools and wash your hands and gloves before moving on to work with other plants in the garden. Once you cut into a diseased plant, fungus spores and other harmful pathogens can remain on your pruning shears and on your gloves for days. Prevent spreading the fungus to healthier plants by disinfecting your tools and gloves and washing your hands after working with damaged plants. A simple wipe of an isopropyl alcohol pad will do the trick.

Common Pests & Treatments

Here are some additional ways to control specific pests that are common in a backyard garden.

CABBAGE WORMS/SLUGS

If you see cabbage worms or slugs, pick them off and destroy them. In addition, another great natural method for control is to use all-purpose flour and dust the plants in the early morning when the plants are still wet from the dew. They will ingest the flour and eventually die.

Crushed eggshells on the ground below plants that are being damaged by slugs are helpful in reducing damage. The sharp edges of the eggshell spells instant death for the slugs as they attempt to crawl over them.

JAPANESE BEETLES

Japanese beetles emerge from the ground in the warmer months and have a life span of three to four weeks. Although they prefer to hang out in rose bushes, Japanese beetles can also be seen eating the foliage of your vegetable plants. If not removed, they will eat the leafy structure of your plants, leaving only the remaining skeleton. The best way to get rid of them is to handpick them off the plant and place them in a small bucket filled with water and dish soap. Wait until they die and discard away from the garden area.

Do not use popular beetle bag traps. They attract beetles from the surrounding area and your garden will be filled with them.

TOMATO HORNWORMS

Tomato hornworms come from the eggs of the sphinx moth, also known as a hawk or hummingbird moth. They lay their eggs on the underside of tomato plants in the spring and, a few weeks later, a green caterpillar with a horn on its end will emerge. You will notice that your tomato plant foliage has been eaten or you will see large green droppings on your plants. You must search for the hornworm on the underside of the leaves. They can be difficult to find, as they camouflage themselves well under the green leaves.

Handpick and destroy each worm, or place it in a bucket of soapy water. Be sure to check daily for hornworm damage. If you see a hornworm that looks like it has little white eggs on its back, leave him in your garden. Those eggs are those of a predatory wasp and will naturally kill the hornworm. These wasps are beneficial to have in your garden for natural pest control.

WHITE MOTHS

The White Moth is the producer of the eggs of cabbage worms. They prefer to land on the Brassica family plants (cabbage, broccoli, Brussels sprouts) and lay their eggs on the underside of the leaves. Once those eggs hatch, the worms are present and begin to eat the foliage. It is difficult to catch the moths by hand as they fly through your garden, however you may find a badminton racket can easily swat them down.

Dealing with Animals

FENCING

As with any garden, the best method of preventing animals from mowing down your crops is to put a fence around it. Although this is not a completely fail-proof way in preventing all animals from finding their way to your vegetable plants, it may deter some to find a new source of food.

During your first garden season, if you find that you have small animals such as groundhogs or rabbits that are creeping into your garden, a small, temporary fence might be needed. Of course, if larger animals such as deer are intruding, a much taller fence will be necessary.

The type of fence that you will need is dependent on the type of animals that are entering your garden. Chicken wire can be wrapped around the bottom perimeter of your fence and secured with stakes for larger, ground-dwelling animals such as groundhogs and large rabbits. However, if you have smaller animals such as chipmunks, squirrels and baby bunnies feasting on your garden, you may find that a solid fence panel made from wood, steel, or concrete block is your only option.

Deer can jump over many types of fences, so you may have to add a top fence cover if your land is subject to frequent visits by deer.

Welded wire mesh or snow fence secured with tall stakes will deter most animals from entering your garden.

Fencing might not always be a feasible option, so let's take a look at a few other strategies to help deter animals away from your first-year garden.

HANG MOTION ITEMS AROUND YOUR GARDEN

Place unexpected movement objects in your garden. Although it may not look the best, placing brightly colored helium balloons around your garden or hanging aluminum pans might just be enough to startle the animals. You may have to switch up the type of object in your garden every few weeks, as the animals may get accustomed to the movement and begin to forage once again.

REPELLENT SPRAY

Using a natural spray on the foliage of your plants is an excellent way to deter animals from eating from the garden. The key to using repellent spray is to apply it early in the morning to prevent burning any plant foliage. You will need to re-spray every five to seven days and after any rainfall.

Of course, you could purchase repellent spray at any garden center, however that can become costly. It is easy to make your own spray at home. Below are two popular homemade repellant sprays and the recipes for making each.

HOT PEPPER SPRAY

Hot pepper spray is an effective tool to deter rabbits, rodents, groundhogs, raccoons and deer from munching on your plants. Spray it on the foliage of your plants, and when the animal goes to take a bite, they get an extremely horrible taste in their mouth and will stop eating your plants.

Mix 1 gallon (3.75 liters) of water and 3 tablespoons (18 grams) of hot pepper flakes in a large saucepan. Bring to a boil, reduce heat and simmer for fifteen minutes. Heating the liquid helps to infuse the oils from the hot peppers into the water, making for a more potent spray.

Let the mixture sit overnight, and then strain through a cheesecloth or micro strainer. Add in a couple of drops of natural, biodegradable dish soap or 1 tablespoon (15 milliliters) of olive oil or milk to the mix. The soap, olive oil or milk additive is nothing more than a "sticking" agent to help the mix adhere to the leaves.

Spray on the foliage of the plants. Repeat spraying every five to seven days or after it rains.

EGG AND MILK SPRAY

This is one of the most time-tested and trusted natural garden sprays for repelling deer and small animals in the garden.

Blend 2 eggs, 4 cloves of garlic, 2 teaspoons (6 grams) of red pepper flakes and ¼ cup (59 milliliters) of whole milk in a blender. Add the mixture to 1 gallon (3.75 liters) of water and mix well. Strain the mixture, and apply the resultant liquid to the foliage of plants where deer, rabbits and other animals have been eating.

Apply the spray every five to seven days and after it rains.

Weed Management

The biggest fear for most gardeners is the thought of weeds overtaking the garden mid-summer. Using the Raised Row Garden method eliminates the never-ending chore of weeding the garden.

Because the entire garden is covered in a protective layer of mulch, weeds have a difficult time seeding themselves. In addition, with the thick layer of mulch in the walking and growing rows, weeds already present in the soil have a difficult time pushing up out of the ground.

Your first layer of mulch, applied during the first season of the Raised Row Garden, will have a tremendous impact on reducing weeds. It will not, however, eliminate all of them. There might be stubborn thistles or dandelions that find a small crack in your mulch during the first year and come to the surface.

The simple way to deal with these weeds in a Raised Row Garden is to remove the few that come up, and continue to apply layers of mulch directly on top of them. The original layers of mulch will have begun to break down, and adding additional mulch will help suppress the weeds. Add additional mulch as needed for complete coverage of the walking rows.

You can also add additional mulch to your growing row zones as needed. If weeds begin to pop up between your plants, add more mulch. Eventually the weeds will not have enough sunlight and oxygen to be able to survive.

The goal is to minimize the time and labor for the gardener by suppressing weeds through mulching.

As the garden season progresses, you may also notice weeds that attempt to grow on the top of your mulch. These weeds, which are brought in by the wind or by birds, send out long, spindly roots to try to reach the soil. Fortunately for the gardener, they can't penetrate through the thick layers of mulch to become established. Simply handpick them off the top of the mulch as you walk by and discard them. No need to for a trowel or shovel, they will come out with just a slight tug.

You will be amazed at how your weed issues dwindle with each successive year.

WHEN TO HARVEST

Knowing when to pick your vegetables is somewhat of a trial and error art. Just because a vegetable is ripe, it doesn't necessarily mean that is the perfect time to pinch it off the vine or pick it off the branch. There are times that you will want to harvest vegetables when they are younger and tenderer than if they were fully ripened. That is purely a personal choice based on your taste preference.

There are some general rules for when to harvest based on the type of plants that you have grown. It is best to pick all vegetable plants early in the morning. The vegetables have had time to rest in the garden overnight, replenishing any water lost from the previous day. The sweeter vegetables use this time to make sugars, and those vegetables harvested in the morning are sweeter, crisper and juicier than those picked at other times.

For leafy crops, such as lettuce, spinach, arugula and kale, you will want to cut their leaves before they get full-sized and taste bitter. Younger, smaller greens taste much milder and sweeter than when they get older. Harvesting them young also encourages additional growth for larger yields. It is best to harvest salad greens in the early morning when the dew is still on the leaves. For best flavor, be sure to pick the greens on the day that you plan to eat them.

Asparagus and quick-growing root crops, like radishes, are best to pick while young. If left to ripen to full potential, they begin to split and/or taste woody.

Vine crops including beans, cucumbers, peas, squash and zucchini, are all best to be picked when they are younger for a tenderer vegetable crop. If left to grow large, cucumbers, zucchini and squash will develop large seed cavities, which are undesirable for consumption. It is best to pick these crops in the early morning, but after the dew has dried to prevent damage to the tender leaves.

Tomatoes, on the other hand, are best left on the vine until ripened whenever possible. Pick them in early morning after the dew has dried. If you notice that pests or animals are damaging your ripe tomatoes, it is best to remove them from the vine prior to being fully ripe to avoid damage and to maximize your yields.

Garlic and onion plants will tell you when they are ready to be picked. Their leaves will begin dying off, and when more than half of them have fallen to the ground, they are ready to be pulled.

Although new potatoes can be dug from the ground at any time during the growing season, it is best to leave larger potato varieties in the ground until the foliage dies off.

As you can see, there are variables on when to harvest, even within the same plant varieties. It is best to educate yourself on the specific type of plant that you planted and when they should be picked. Keep in mind that picking vegetables early and often encourages the plant to produce more.

THE TEN MINUTE A DAY APPROACH TO GARDEN MAINTENANCE

The whole purpose of starting a Raised Row Garden is to work smarter, not harder. Once you get through year one, your time and effort to maintain a Raised Row Garden will be minimal, and the quality and quantity of your yields will only improve.

However, it is important to note that a little bit of garden maintenance on a daily basis goes a long way. Spend just a little time each and every day walking through and maintaining your Raised Row Garden, and you will end up with a beautiful and easy-to-maintain garden!

Spending ten minutes each day in the garden is not the same as 70 minutes once a week. It may be mathematically, but not from an end-result standpoint. If you let your garden space go for days at a time, small weeds can turn into a jungle, and hornworms can destroy a tomato plant or two. However, if you are in the garden for at least ten minutes each day, you not only can detect any potential issue, but also take care of it before the task becomes out of control. Water, add mulch, inspect your plants, pull the occasional weed or just enjoy the peace and tranquility of your new garden space.

CHAPTER 7

COMPOST AND COMPOSTING

Creating Black Gold to Power the Raised Row Garden

Without a doubt, compost is the star of the show when it comes to powering the Raised Row Garden.

There is a reason many gardeners use the term "black gold" when referring to compost. Its value to a garden's vitality and richness is comparable to the worth of the shiny mineral that has been sought out since humans first roamed the earth.

We use compost in every single phase of our growing process, from planting, to mulching, to making our own liquid fertilizer. It's free, it's all-natural and it works! See page 100 for instructions on making compost teas and page 127 for step-by-step plans to complete your very own compost bin.

Compost teems with a vast array of microbes, organisms and minerals needed to power big yields from vegetable plants. The best part of all, unlike real gold, is that a near-endless supply of black gold can be made right in your backyard—for free!

Compost is certainly not a new or novel idea. In fact, it has been used in some shape or form to help grow food by nearly every culture, dating back to well before the Roman Empire.

It really wasn't until the last 75 years or so that the practice of using compost and other natural soil-building techniques began to be replaced by inexpensive and readily available man-made fertilizers. But what seemed to be a good idea at the time has now raised a lot of questions about health, sustainability and issues such as fertilizer runoff to lakes and ponds, endangering both wildlife and our drinking water.

Composting, on the other hand, is a simple, natural process. It is also the best way to add nutrient-rich humus to your Raised Row Garden, boosting both plant growth and productivity, all while adding depleted nutrients back into the soil.

THE BENEFITS OF MAKING YOUR OWN COMPOST

Although you can purchase finished compost at most garden stores, it can get quite expensive for a backyard garden. And to supply needed amounts for a Raised Row Garden, it simply makes sense, as in dollars and cents, to create your own.

Making your own compost has zero cost, is simple to make and keeps the environment healthy in a variety of ways. It also fits hand-in-hand with the sustainable approach that Raised Row Gardening brings to growing your own vegetables. Compost really is king. To drive home the point, just take a look at a few of the benefits home composting can bring to you and your garden.

Eliminates the Need for Commercial Fertilizers

Commercial fertilizers not only cost a fortune, but also, over time, deplete the soil's structure and affect other beneficial nutrients in the soil. The end result is a need for even more chemicals and synthetic fertilizers to balance it all out. It's an expensive and questionable cycle that can be eliminated by simply replenishing soil with your own nutrient-rich compost each year.

Read the label of a synthetic fertilizer product and you will find that almost all application instructions include that you should wear personal protective equipment when applying it to your garden. Ever see commercial farmers spraying fields? They are required to wear masks and gloves and, in some cases, a respirator to prevent them from inhaling dangerous fumes.

With composting, there is no need for masks or goggles, and even gloves are optional when applying it throughout the garden.

The fact is, by working generous amounts of compost into your garden, you can all but eliminate the need to ever use synthetic fertilizers or chemicals again. The bottom line—making your own compost is a huge money saver.

Cuts Down on Household Waste

By simply composting the waste of the food products currently consumed in the household, you can eliminate a large portion of your weekly trash pick-up.

As an example, think of just a typical morning routine for most households. Yesterday's coffee grounds and paper filter go into the trash to make way for a fresh pot of coffee. Having a few eggs for breakfast? Out go the eggshells. As do the potato peels for that morning's plate of hash browns, fried potatoes or potato cakes. And with it, the melon or grapefruit rinds, orange peels or other fruit remnants left behind. These are all food scraps that would have ended up in the trash, and eventually a landfill, but now can power your garden!

It is truly amazing how much the simple act of composing can cut down on your weekly trash. When we first started composting in 2010, we reduced our weekly trash by more than half!

Recycles Valuable Yard Waste

Much like household kitchen scraps, many yard waste products could be used instead to build and power an incredible compost pile.

The most obvious of all is bagged autumn leaves. Just drive around a suburban neighborhood in September, and you will see mountains of black or paper trash bags piled up on the curb filled with leaves. These leaves don't need to go to a landfill; they need to go to your compost pile!

There are all types of yard waste materials that should be recycled into compost, including plant and shrub trimmings, grass clippings, dead flowers, spent foliage, dead garden plants and vegetables that have been kept free of disease. Keeping these out of landfills not only helps to save our environment, but also will create an amazingly fertile garden when turned into the black gold of compost!

Provides Natural Pest and Disease Control for Your Garden

In addition to the rich humus, minerals and compounds found in compost, there are several beneficial organisms present in compost that provide natural pest and disease control for your garden soil.

Homemade compost is the perfect home for earthworms, which will in turn be added to your raised rows. The combination of microscopic organisms and earthworms within your homemade compost will help aerate the soil, provide ideal planting conditions, deter unwanted ground pests and ward off plant disease.

KEEPING COMPOSTING SIMPLE—THE BASICS

Composting doesn't need to be a complicated process. Unfortunately, the overload of technical information dispensed by the composting "experts" discourages many who think about making their own compost quickly.

One quick online search for composting methods can leave your head spinning with all the various dos and don'ts.

And that leads to perhaps the best piece of advice in this entire chapter: Remember that, with or without human intervention to provide "the perfect" environment, all things in nature will eventually decompose, including your backyard compost pile!

For the overwhelming wealth of information on the importance of the exact and perfect ratios of carbon materials, nitrogen sources or moisture levels in your pile, remember, first and foremost, decomposition is a natural process. Everything eventually composts. Yes, there are indeed ways to make it faster, and we feature many of those simple methods below, but the most important thing of all is to not get so caught up in the confusion of ratios and details that you never get around to starting a compost pile. No pile means no compost. And with a Raised Row Garden, you need compost!

Creating a Compost Pile from Scratch

Let's start from the beginning when it comes to compost.

At its very core, a good compost pile starts with the proper balance of brown (carbon) and green (nitrogen) materials. Think of the browns as the more lifeless of the two, while the greens are the vibrant, fresh and active portion of the mix.

Brown materials consist of leaves, straw, wood shavings, dead grass, small twigs and limbs.

Greens include materials like vegetable peels, coffee grounds, green grass clippings and fresh plant or garden clippings. Greens also include animal by-products like chicken, rabbit, horse and cow manure.

Below is a breakdown of some of the most commonly added compost materials and where they fall on the brown versus green scale.

BROWN CARBON-BASED MATERIALS	GREEN NITROGEN-BASED MATERIALS
shredded dried leaves	vegetable scraps
straw	fruit scraps
shrub prunings—cut in small pieces	coffee grounds with filter
pine needles	cow, horse, chicken and rabbit manure
sawdust	flower cuttings
wood ash	fresh grass clippings
corn cobs/stalks	garden plant foliage—disease free
non-glossy newspaper	seaweed
shredded paper	tea bags
cardboard	eggshells
dryer lint	nut shells

Here is where it can get complicated. This is where many composting experts will tell you about complicated ratios of carbon to nitrogen sources, based on the dry weight of the materials added. They come up with the ratios using all sorts of complicated equations, and you can quickly lose your mind trying to follow them verbatim.

In place of all of these complicated equations, we use a simple composting rule of thumb: For every four to five parts of brown material (carbon) added to a compost pile, add one part green (nitrogen).

For example, if adding a 1-gallon (3.75 kilogram) bucket of coffee grounds and vegetable scraps collected from the kitchen, 4 to 5 gallons (15 to 19 kilograms) of shredded leaves, straw or other fibrous materials need to be added as well. If you are adding in chicken manure (green) cleaned out a coop, you need to add four to five times as much brown material to the pile.

Don't get lost in trying to be exact. These are basic ratios to help any pile decompose at a reasonable rate. This one simple, but effective, rule of thumb has produced load after load of great compost for our garden year after year, and it will work for you as well.

If you get a little out of balance, the pile will still break down, just not as quickly. As you progress with your composting skills, you will begin to get a feel for when a pile is a bit out of whack, and you can easily take measures to fix it.

If you notice your pile has become extremely dry and lifeless, it may simply have too much of a carbon consistency to heat up and decompose at a fast rate. Add greens and mix them in to provide a better balance.

On the other hand, if your pile has become more on the slimy side, with a strong, pungent odor, add a little more of the browns.

Composting Materials to Avoid

When it comes to backyard composting, there are a few materials you will want to avoid, both to deter animals and to help with the long-term health of your pile and garden.

Meat and fish products, cooked foods, cooking oils or oily food remnants, diseased or unhealthy plants, weeds or invasive plant material, dog or cat feces, pressure treated wood shavings and sawdust should all be avoided.

Although meats and oils can be successfully composted in high temperature piles, for the average gardener, these spell trouble. They bring in unwanted vermin such as raccoons, possums, mice and rats. Adding to the problem, these materials can produce an awful smell as they decompose.

When it comes to weeds that have gone to seed, they are best left out of the home compost pile. Most compost piles will not get hot enough to kill weed seeds as they decompose, and they end up planted back in the garden when you apply your compost to your raised rows.

Cat and dog feces (and human feces, for that matter) may contain disease that cannot be destroyed during the composting process. These should NEVER be used. By adding the feces to the compost pile, you risk passing on harmful organisms to you and your family via the harvested vegetables.

Lumber or lumber products like sawdust, wood shavings and small wood chips should only be added if they have not been treated.

How to Create the Right-Sized Compost Pile

When it comes to creating your compost pile, a little lesson gleaned from Goldilocks and the Three Bears can be quite helpful. If your compost pile is too small, your materials will never "heat up" enough to decompose quickly. If the pile is too big, it becomes difficult to turn and mix, and that can slow things down as well. Get it just right, and great things happen!

For best results, keep the size of your pile to a minimum of 3 by 3 by 3 feet (1 by 1 by 1 meter) and a maximum of 5 by 5 by 5 feet (1.5 by 1.5 by 1.5 meters).

CHOP-CHOP

The smaller the material going in to the pile, the quicker it will decompose.

If you have large quantities of leaves, shred them up with the lawnmower before adding. The same goes for kitchen scraps. A few more chops with your knife before throwing them in helps them break down more quickly and will speed up the decomposition process. A quick pulse or two in the food processor or blender can be helpful for this, too.

The more surface areas exposed to heat and microorganisms of the pile, the more quickly a pile begins to break down. Chopping and cutting ingredients prior to placing in the pile is a must for fast composting.

Turning your compost pile frequently keeps vital oxygen supplied to the inner core of the pile. Without it, compost piles cannot heat to the temperatures required for efficient decomposition.

TURN BABY TURN

Much like we need oxygen to survive, the organisms that help to break down your compost pile need air to thrive. By turning your pile with a spade or pitchfork, you keep the pile alive and well and your pile cooking. The compost on the outer edges of the pile will be the coolest and driest. Use your pitchfork or shovel to turn this material over and place it in the middle of your pile. This allows air into the center of the pile, and lets the materials that were on the outer edges have a chance to break down faster while being moved to the hot center.

Proper moisture is a key component to a healthy compost pile. You may need to add water to your pile during extremely hot or dry periods of weather.

Turning your pile daily is the best way to keep compost cooking quickly. Make it a habit during your daily ten minutes in the garden to grab your pitchfork or shovel and turn the pile.

At the very least, be sure to turn your compost pile a few times a week to keep the heat and decomposition process at optimum levels.

KEEP THE PILE MOIST

Moisture is the final key to a great compost pile. If the pile dries out, the center will begin to cool and decomposition will slow to a crawl. Too much water causes the same cooling effect, and the pile has trouble finding oxygen.

So how much is enough? A good rule to follow here is that a pile should have the consistency and moisture of a well-wrung sponge—damp, but not dripping.

Each time you turn the pile, keep an eye on the moisture level. If you notice it beginning to dry out, add a little water to bring up the moisture content. If you have trouble regulating the moisture due to excessive rain or heat, cover the pile with a sheet, a canvas tarp or a large piece of plastic. It will help keep moisture in during hot days and prevent it from becoming drenched during heavy downpours.

WHERE TO FIND COMPOST MATERIALS FOR FREE

Whether you compost in 5-gallon (19-liter) buckets, fancy bins, barrels or in a huge pile "out back" finding the resources to fill your pile should never be a problem.

The first step is to find out what you have in your own home and yard that could be added to your compost bin. There are some easily accessible items such as vegetable and fruit scraps, coffee, tea, paper and even dryer lint. However, there are times that you are going to need additional materials that aren't found in the quantities that you need them, if at all.

So where can you obtain items for your compost for free? We have listed the most common solutions to obtaining free composting materials. The only cost involved is the time spent in asking and collecting!

Autumn Leaves and Clean-Up Time

Autumn is the easiest time to gather free materials for the compost bin. If you don't have your own leaves to collect, simply drive around a suburban neighborhood for an endless supply of leaves for your pile. Most of the time, they are already bagged at the curbside for easy pick-up. Although they are at the curbside for collection by the garbage company, it is best to ask the homeowner if you can take them. Although it may appear that the bags are full of leaves, they may also contain unwanted trash or personal items that were meant for the landfill.

If the homeowners are willing to give you already-raked bags of leaves, take as many as you can store! They will be a great addition to your compost pile immediately, store well and will supply you with additional materials later in the year, when needed.

Some leaves are better for composting than others. Maple, birch, ash, beech and fruit tree leaves make a great addition to your compost pile in unlimited quantities. Oak leaves, on the other hand, should be composted in moderation or for long periods of time, as they have a high acidity level that can result in compost that is less than ideal for most vegetable gardens. The goal is to provide no more than 20 percent of your compost pile in oak leaves to ensure that it is safe to apply on your raised rows.

Do not place whole leaves in your compost bin. They first must be shredded to prevent layers of leaves matting together and creating a barrier in your compost pile. A simple swipe of a push lawn mower across your leaves will adequately shred them. This will also help speed up the decomposition of the leaves and make a hot compost pile.

Another great source of compost materials in the fall is outdoor decorations. Companies and individuals that decorate for harvest fests and Thanksgiving suddenly have no use for those straw bales, pumpkins, gourds and corn stalks by the end of November. Just ask the owner if you can pick them up on a mutually agreed-upon date so they don't have to dispose of them. This is a terrific way to get straw into your compost pile that would otherwise be decomposing in a landfill.

Cafes, Diners and Restaurants

Most breakfast restaurants use dozens of eggs, potatoes and coffee each day, leaving an opportunity for you to collect their empty eggshells, vegetable peels, coffee grounds and filters to add to your compost pile. The best place to ask is at a locally-owned, smaller-sized café or diner. Explain what you would like for them to collect, and make it easy on them by providing them with 5-gallon (19-liter) buckets with lids. It is important to collect them within a day or two to prevent any health issues at the restaurant.

Coffee Shops

Many local, regional and even national chain coffee shops such as Starbucks are typically more than happy to put their coffee grounds to good use by saving them for their customers. Some shops even create a list of customers that they save their grounds for and post it on a chalkboard wall to promote that their by-product doesn't end up in the landfill.

Even if your coffee shop doesn't already have a sign posted, ask the store staff if they will save the grounds for you. And be sure to let them know there is no need to separate the grounds from the filters. Both the grounds and filters will decompose quickly in your pile.

Grocery Stores and Produce Stands

Small grocery stores and produce stands can be a goldmine for obtaining composting materials. Many large, chain grocery stores already provide non-profit organizations with their over-ripened fruits and vegetables and may not have the ability to help out individuals. However, smaller grocery stores, especially ones that have a nice selection of organic materials, are usually more than happy to help out a customer that shops at their store or produce stand.

All it takes is a quick conversation with the owner or manager to find out what is currently done with expired produce and to ask them if they could save them for you. Those rotten tomatoes, potatoes and fruit may be past their prime to sell in the store, but they make great additions to any compost pile. Again, it is important to make it easy on the provider by supplying them with buckets and picking them up at an agreed-upon time.

Landscapers and Tree Companies

Contact local landscapers and tree-trimming companies to investigate what they do with the trees that they shred down. Many times, they have to pay a fee or travel a long way to dump them at a mulch facility. If they are in your neighborhood completing work, or if they drive by your area frequently, ask them to drop off a load at your house. You'll be surprised how many are more than happy to accommodate you with tons of shredded goodness, for free, and drop it off right at your doorstep.

Local Horse Stables, Hobby Farms and Farmers

Many local, hobby farmers and owners of small horse stables are more than glad to give away their manure to gardeners. The high nitrogen sources in chicken, cow, horse and rabbit manure helps to heat your pile to make quick compost. In addition, most manure will contain bedding materials such as straw or wood shavings that add additional benefits to your compost mixture.

Most farmers will let you take the manure as long as you have a way to take it home. Be prepared to shovel it yourself, and, if you don't have a truck, a few 5-gallon (19-liter) buckets with lids will be beneficial to your backyard compost pile. For those that worry about the smell or odor of livestock manure, once you blend the manure in the compost pile little to no odor can be detected.

It is important to remember that fresh manure is not safe to use in a growing garden. Fresh animal manure contains a high level of acidity and nitrogen that must be neutralized and diluted during the composting process. It must be composted for six months prior to use around growing vegetable plants.

Neighbors and Friends

Friends and neighbors can be a great resource when you are trying to get volumes of materials to start composting. Neighbors who live in close proximity to you are easily accessible and are typically willing to help out. They, like you, eat fruits and vegetables, drink their morning coffee or tea and have to mow their lawn.

COMPOSTING CONTAINERS

There is a near-endless supply of composting vessels available to create and make compost. You can compost in barrels, bins and drums of all shapes and sizes. In fact, it seems like every time you turn around, there is a new composting container hitting the market!

So what are the best choices? Although all containers will work on some level, the perfect compost vessel will be large enough to accommodate a pile that can heat up and maintain its power. To accomplish that, you need a pile, or some type of container that is at least 3 by 3 feet (1 by 1 meters). We use a two-bin compost system in our home garden, and it really works wonders. Each bin is 3 by 3 feet (1 by 1 meters), and they sit side by side. While one side holds an active pile, we use the second bin to hold finished compost for everyday use. As our finished pile is depleted, we let the active pile finish off, and start a new pile in the old, finished compost bin. This keeps a perpetual pile of compost active at all times, with easy access to finished compost when needed.

HOW TO CREATE YOUR OWN COMPOST BIN

We have used our homemade two-bin compost container to make load after load of black gold to power our garden! It's simple to make, and looks great in nearly any setting.

Tape measure

Screw gun

Saw (hand saw, circular saw, jigsaw or chop saw)

10 pieces 1 by 4 by 10 feet (.25 by 1.25 by 3 meters) untreated lumber, cut into 39 pieces that are each 30 inches (76 cm) long

5 pieces 2 by 4 by 10 feet (0.5 by 1.25 by 3 meters) untreated lumber, cut into the following lengths: 2 (72-inch [2-meter]) pieces, 9 (27-inch [69-cm]) pieces, 6 (30-inch [76-cm]) pieces

40 (2½-inch [6-cm]) screws or nails

50 (1½-inch [4-cm]) screws or nails

1. On a level surface, place the two 72-inch (2-meter) 2 by 4 pieces on the ground 28 inches (71 cm) apart. Turn each piece on its side so that the larger 4-inch (10-cm) area is not touching the ground. Place a 27-inch (69-cm) 2 by 4 board on the inside edge of each end, with the larger 4-inch (10-cm) side of the board not touching the ground. Screw the top and bottom of each board using two 2½-inch (6-cm) screws on each joint. Using the same method to attach the end boards, place a third 27-inch (69-cm) board in the center of your rectangular frame and screw into place. When assembled, your front frame will be 6 feet wide by 30 inches (76 cm) high.

2. Make three smaller frames using two 30-inch (76-cm) boards for the top and bottom and two 27-inch (69-cm) boards for each side, using the same technique as above. Repeat this process until all three smaller frames have been assembled.

3. Assemble each of the three smaller frames to the large rectangular front frame. Place on the outer edges of the large frame and place six 2½-inch (6-cm) screws to secure it (two on top, two in the middle, two on the bottom). Assemble the third small square directly in the middle of the frame, attaching it in the center of the middle support of the front frame.

(continued)

HOW TO CREATE YOUR OWN COMPOST BIN (CONTINUED)

4. Using 1½-inch (4-cm) screws: Starting on the front side place fifteen 1 by 4 by 30 boards along the front, evenly spacing the boards with the two end boards evenly aligned with the each side leaving ½ inch (1 cm) between boards. The spacing is necessary so that your compost bin can receive adequate airflow.

5. Complete the same assembly of the slats on each end frame using eight 1 by 4 by 30 on each side and on the center frame, leaving ¼ inch (0.5 cm) between boards.

6. Place your two-bin compost holder onto a level surface directly on top of the earth.

Sheet Composting and Hole Composting

Although compost bins are truly the ideal medium for composting, there are two alternatives if you simply do not have the necessary space—Sheet Composting and Hole Composting.

SHEET COMPOSTING

Sheet composting can be completed in the fall and uses a unique layering method by applying both carbon and nitrogen organic materials on top of each other directly in your raised rows. This technique allows the use of abundant leaves that are readily available in the fall. Sheet compost can be applied in the raised rows where you will not be adding an over-winter cover crop, such as your small seed beds, for next year's garden.

Remove spent plants from the garden. In the growing row zone, alternate 1-inch (2.5-cm) layers of carbon and nitrogen materials. A sample may look like: kitchen scraps in the first layer, shredded leaves in the second, grass clippings in the third, straw in the fourth and chicken manure in the last, top layer. Each layer should be at least 1-inch (2.5-cm) thick.

This is the one time that you can place fresh livestock manure directly in your garden bed. This is possible because the manure will break down with the other composting materials over winter and be safe for planting in the spring.

Make sure to place an organic material on the top layer that will not blow away. Let the layers decompose over winter, and by spring you'll have a fully composted raised row bed ready for planting.

Whether you make your own or purchase, compost is an absolute necessity for the long-term success of the organic Raised Row Garden! Not only does it build incredible soil, but also it provides the basis for compost tea, the all-purpose natural fertilizer for the garden.

HOLE COMPOSTING

Hole composting can be practiced nearly any time of year that the ground can be worked. It is an excellent option for those with little space.

Hole composting is the process of burying compostable materials directly into the growing soil. In a Raised Row Garden, this can be done by digging down 10 to 12 inches (25 to 30 cm) in an unused area of a growing row, and burying whatever scraps and remnants you have. These remnants will break down over time, enriching the soil as they do.

In season, when plants are growing, be sure to locate any trench holes at least 12 inches (30 cm) from the base of existing plants to keep from disturbing the root system.

CHAPTER 8

THE RAISED ROW GARDEN IN FALL

Fall is a busy time in the garden, especially when it comes to a Raised Row Garden. Not only do you have a second chance at planting cooler-weather loving and over-wintering crops, but also you will be harvesting the bounty of the produce from the main summer garden.

In addition to planting and harvesting chores, the process of clearing out the first of the past season's crop begins. Some will be cleared out to make way for those second chance and over-wintering crops, while others can be put away to rest and recharge by planting a cover crop or a protective and soil-building covering of winter mulch.

Which rows receive what covering are all part of your crop rotation and planting plan. We will cover those topics in-depth in Chapter 10. For now, let's take a closer look at the specific chores in the fall Raised Row Garden—second chance plantings, planting over-wintering crops and harvesting existing plantings.

PLANTING A SECOND ROUND OF CROPS

What can be planted in a fall vegetable garden will greatly depend on where you live. Gardeners who live in hot, tropical climates with mild fall and winter temperatures have an opportunity to finally plant vegetables like tomatoes, peppers and eggplant. These varieties struggle in the excessive heat of summer, but fall presents the perfect opportunity to grow these plants without the worry of the sun and heat wilting and destroying the foliage and blooms.

However, for many gardeners who live in areas that have more typical, cooler fall temperatures, the second crop plant choices lend themselves toward the fast-growing, cool-loving and quick-to-mature crops that worked well in the early spring.

Vegetables such as leafy greens, radishes, cabbage and broccoli are all perfect for planting in the Raised Row Garden of a traditional four-season style climate. As are a second crop of green beans, sugar snap peas, cucumbers and nearly all annual herbs.

Many of the spring and early summer vegetables have started to wane by late summer, and as one plant is done producing, it can be pulled from the ground to make way for a second planting of fall vegetables in its place. Most of these plants can be easily sown via seed, although there are a few that perform better as transplants.

Fall Plantings from Seed

Starting a second round of crops via seed in the late summer or early fall has many advantages over spring-time gardening.

The warmer air and soil temperatures are ideal for quickly sprouting seeds. Late summer and fall gardens also typically don't battle the severe temperature swings that early spring plantings face. This more consistent temperature leads to better seed germination and plant health.

In addition, many pests and disease issues that thrive in the wet, cooler temperatures of early spring fade away as the heat of late summer and early fall settle in.

Fall seeds need to be planted a bit deeper than their spring counterparts. This helps to keep the seeds from drying out too quickly from the warmer soil and air temperatures.

Keep in mind that what you plant in the fall will need to fully mature before the first frost. Many plants will grow well in cool weather, but need to be started while the soil is still warm in late summer or early fall, and while the days are hot and long enough to get the plant well-established before the cooler nights arrive. Although hardiness maps are a good place to start to determine your first and last frost dates, check with your local extension office to find out more exact first average frost dates for your specific location.

When seeding directly into the soil, choose vegetable varieties that mature in the shortest amount of time. Some cucumber seeds will mature in as quickly as 50 days, while others won't be ready to harvest until 75 days after planting.

The best way to determine the length of time that you have for a fall garden season is to count back from your first average frost date and plant accordingly.

PLANT A LITTLE DEEPER

Although you will prepare your seed trenches the same way as during spring planting, plant fall seeds ½-inch (1-cm) deeper than what the package recommends. Unfortunately, seed packet directions are generally geared toward spring planting. When planting in the spring, the seeds can be placed more near the surface to benefit from the soil warming from the sun.

By late summer, the soil at the top can be too warm for germination, and can dry out too quickly. Planting deeper allows the seed to find cooler soil and proper moisture to germinate.

Fall Plantings from Transplants

There are a few fall crops that are best placed in your garden as transplants. Cabbage, broccoli and cauliflower all need roughly three months to mature from seed, and are simply not ideal to grow from seed by the time fall has arrived.

However, they all thrive in cool weather. By planting six-week-old transplants in the ground, you can cut off a few weeks of growing time. Start seeds for these plants in pots outdoors six weeks before you will plant in the ground. By starting seeds in pots, you can keep the young, tender seedlings in the shade or in cooler areas on extremely hot days. If you were to plant these seeds directly in the hot, summer soil, they would struggle to survive.

You can also, of course, purchase sprouted seedlings at a local garden center, although the selection for fall transplants is usually sparser than in the springtime. Simply plant them in your garden when the designated raised row becomes available.

Whether you plant the seeds directly in the ground or plant transplants, you must provide your newly-planted fall garden with adequate water to become established. Often, spring rains help these crops become established and promote quick growth. The heat of a mid to late summer planting can cause stress on spring crops. Transplants can handle swings in temperature and various water quantities better than directly planted seeds. Water generously as needed to ensure a bountiful fall harvest.

FALL CROPS

Let's take a look at how to best plant the most common fall crops in the Raised Row Garden.

ARUGULA

Arugula often grows better in the fall than in spring. In spring, the plant often becomes too hot and is quick to produce flowers and seeds. But in fall, when days become cooler, the plants are able to use their effort and energy to produce a bounty of edible leaves. Plant arugula seeds ¼ to ½ inch (0.5 to 1 cm) deep spaced 4 to 6 inches (10 to 15 cm) apart in three furrows. They will sprout within a week if the raised row bed is moist. Continue to add mulch as needed to improve the soil moisture and to enhance growth. Harvest any time the leaves are greater than 2 inches (5 cm) in height by cutting the leaves. This will encourage additional growth throughout the fall season.

BEETS

Beets perform well in both the spring and fall and do grow well in the summer. They can handle light frost and will continue to grow until the first hard freeze. Beets are ideal to grow in succession for an extended harvest season that can last until winter. Plant seeds 2 inches (5 cm) apart, ½- to ¾-inch (1- to 2-cm) deep in four furrows. Plant seeds every two weeks until six weeks before the first frost date.

BROCCOLI

Planting broccoli in the fall has two big advantages over spring planting. Spring broccoli seedlings are not as hardy as fall seedlings, and early spring frosts can stunt their growth or even kill them. Fall broccoli florets are slower to open in the cool weather, allowing you additional time to harvest before flowering. Although broccoli plants can withstand light frost, it is best to plant quick-growing varieties to allow enough time to harvest before the first hard frost. Plant 18 inches (46 cm) apart in a zig-zag, off-setting formation, for a maximum 24 plants in a 20-foot (6-meter) growing row.

BUSH GREEN BEANS

Bush green beans are quick growers and love the cool conditions of fall. Many varieties will start producing in as little as 45 days, making them perfect to plant for a fall harvest. Be sure to plant them well before the first frost, as bean plants cannot handle even the slightest frost. Plant seeds down two furrows at 1½ inches (4 cm) deep, spaced 3 inches (7.5 cm) apart.

(continued)

FALL CROPS (CONTINUED)

CABBAGE

Fall provides the perfect growing weather for cabbage. The transplants will thrive and grow quickly in the warm weather of late summer, but need the cool nights to form the head. Cabbage plants require a three-month period to mature, so it will be one of the first fall crops that you put in the ground in late summer or early fall. Plant 18 inches (46 cm) apart in a zig-zag, off-setting formation, for a maximum of eighteen plants in a 20-foot (6-meter) growing row.

Cabbage can handle light frosts, but harvest before the first hard freeze for the best flavor. Light frost occurs when nighttime temperatures reach near, or right below, the freezing mark of 32°F (0°C). These temperatures will produce frost on top of the foliage, but not kill hardy plants. A hard freeze usually occurs when temperatures dip into the mid 20°F (-6½°C) range, which is cold enough to kill off even hardy, annual vegetables.

CAULIFLOWER

Cauliflower does extremely well in the fall, and, for most experienced gardeners, fall is the preferred time to plant. The cool weather produces tender cauliflower heads, which normally tend to remain nice and tight. Plant cauliflower transplants at the same time as you plant cabbage, as it does take several weeks to mature. Plant 12 inches (30 cm) apart in a zig-zag, off-setting formation, for a maximum of eighteen plants in a 20-foot (6-meter) growing row.

CILANTRO

Cilantro loves cool weather and will flourish in your fall garden. It is a fast-growing annual and will bolt (go quickly to seed) when the weather gets hot in the spring. During the late summer, plant cilantro seeds just below the surface, 6 to 8 inches (15 to 20 cm) apart, every two weeks to extend your fall harvest. If your cilantro does go to seed, save the seeds (coriander) for use in your winter recipes.

CUCUMBERS

Cucumber seeds will thrive when started in the warm temperatures of mid-summer. The seeds will germinate quickly in the heat of the soil and can produce fruit in as little as 50 days. Planting compact, quick-growing varieties will prevent a threat of an unexpected frost from ending your harvest too soon. Space mounds 30 to 36 inches (76 to 91 cm) apart, placing three seeds in each mound.

GREEN BEANS

Spring-planted green beans are usually heading into their final picking by late July. So, why not plant another crop to enjoy a delicious second round later? With the warm summer soil, bean seeds germinate quickly. Plant your seeds in mid-summer, and you will be enjoying a second crop by September. Plant two furrows with seeds 1½ inches (4 cm) deep, placed 3 inches (7.5 cm) apart.

GREEN ONIONS

Green onions are a quick-growing seed crop and can be ready for harvest in as little as twenty days. If you have open garden space available, you can succession plant every two weeks from mid-summer through the fall. You can also plant green onions in the rows to be cleared in late summer, due to green onions having such a short maturity date. Plant in three furrows with seeds placed ½ inch (1 cm) deep, spaced 3 inches (7.5 cm) apart.

KALE

Kale is one of the easiest fall crops to grow. The seeds are versatile and can tolerate both warm and cool soil temperatures. Plant in three furrows, spacing seeds 4 inches (10 cm) apart at ½-inch (1-cm) depth. Kale leaves will begin to emerge, and you can cut them for use at any height. They will continue to regrow and provide you with greens through the first frost. As the temperatures begin to cool, the kale will become more tender and sweeter, making it a preferred fall leafy green.

LETTUCE

Lettuce grows well in both the spring and fall and does not like hot weather. Fall lettuce will produce a sweeter and crisper flavor as the temperature becomes cooler than in the spring. This is a quick-to-mature seed crop and can be planted in late summer. Plant at ½-inch (1-cm) depth, and spaced ½ to 1 inch (1 to 2.5 cm) apart in up to four furrows. To maximize yields, succession planting every week is recommended, as fall planted lettuce is slower to grow than spring lettuce.

RADISHES

Radishes like to grow quickly and in cool, moist soil. They do well in early spring, but tend to taste woody or bitter by late spring. Fall radishes will provide an excellent taste, but will need a consistent level of moisture to produce plump bulbs. For a constant supply late into fall, plant radish seeds in five furrows at ½-inch (1-cm) depth spaced 1 to 2 inches (2.5 to 5 cm) apart every two weeks, until 30 days before the first frost date.

(continued)

FALL CROPS (CONTINUED)

SPINACH

Planting spinach in the spring can be disappointing. It takes a long time to germinate and can quickly bolt if the spring temperatures get too warm. Fall spinach takes advantage of the warm soil temperatures for germination, using the cooling temperatures to produce tender and tasty leaves. Some spinach varieties mature in just 30 days, and even less if you like small, tender leaves of baby spinach. Plant in three furrows at ½-inch (1-cm) depth, spaced every 4 inches (10 cm). Succession plant spinach seeds every two weeks until 30 days before the first hard freeze. Spinach can tolerate light frosts and provides for a long fall harvest.

SUGAR SNAP/SNOW PEAS

Peas grow well in the spring, but can also be planted for a fall harvest. To determine when to sow your fall crop, check the days to maturity on the back of the seed packet and count backward from the expected first frost date. Directly plant the seeds in two furrows at 1 to 2 inches (2.5 to 5 cm) in depth in the garden, and water. Peas do not like extremely hot temperatures, and their growth will be stunted if exposed to intense direct sunlight. As the plants begin to grow, the cool fall temperatures will be ideal when it is time to flower and form pea pods. Harvest before the first frost.

HELPING THE HARVEST IN THE FALL

Indeterminate tomato plants and slow-growing pepper plants are often still loaded with fruit late into the summer and into early fall. As summer begins to fade and the first frost is nearing, it is time to focus your energy on helping sizeable fruit left on the vine to ripen as much as possible.

Four weeks before the average first frost date, cut off the top portion of each growing stem to encourage all the energy and effort of the plant to ripen the fruit rather than producing new stems and foliage. Pinch off any flowers or small tomatoes or peppers that will not have a chance to become large enough before the cold snap begins.

The day before frost has been predicted and is likely to occur in your area, pick all remaining sizeable fruit for ripening inside. Wrap green tomatoes and peppers in newspaper or place in a closed brown paper bag to speed up the ripening process indoors.

Although green tomatoes aren't desirable to eat raw, you can eat them by frying, stewing or pickling them.

Never allow your annual vegetable plants to over-winter in the soil. Plants that are left to rot and decay can easily spread fungus and disease, as well as harbor harmful insects.

Clear Off Crops

Knowing when to clear out your garden rows is dependent on the type of vegetable varieties that you have grown and the overall health and vitality of the individual plants and crops.

Of course, as a plant dies off it should be removed from the soil. Keep in mind that there are some plants that may look healthy; however, their purpose in the garden has passed.

The next page has three guidelines on when it is time to remove plants from your garden.

WHEN NON-FRUITING PLANTS GO TO FLOWER

When non-fruiting annual plants like greens and root vegetables produce flowers, it is time to pull them out of the garden. This process is commonly known as bolting. The production of the flowers indicates that the vegetable has reached the end of its life-cycle as an edible garden plant. Pull the entire plant out of the garden to prevent seeds from entering the raised rows.

THE PLANT HAS STOPPED PRODUCING FRUIT

There are times when plants have healthy-looking green foliage, but are no longer producing fruit. Determinate tomato varieties produce fruit for a set amount of time, typically for a two- to three-week time period. After that time has passed, the chance for additional fruit to appear is minimal. It is better to pull that plant out of the ground as it weakens to prevent it from attracting pests and diseases.

If your plant hasn't produced well all season long, it could be due to several reasons. Over-fertilization will cause a plant to develop thick green foliage with little to no fruit. Or, the plant could have been a weak plant from the beginning and struggled all season long. Poor pollination can also cause a healthy, flowering plant to never develop fruit. Whatever the reason, if your plant is not producing, remove it from the ground. These plants will continue to deplete your soil of nutrients and will become a breeding ground for pests and diseases looking for a home.

THE PLANT IS BEGINNING TO TURN YELLOW OR BROWN AND LOSING A LOT OF LEAVES

Once annual vegetable foliage begins to yellow or turn brown, and the stems become weak and limp, you can begin to remove the plants from the garden. The timing of a plant dying back will vary from not only variety to variety, but also within the same variety depending on the health and growth of each individual plant.

The process of clearing out plants that are dying off can take many weeks. The best thing to do is pull the plant out before it declines in strength completely to prevent harmful garden bugs and disease from being attracted to your garden.

If the plant material shows any signs of disease, it should be disposed of in the trash or burned. If you compost diseased plant material, you risk re-infecting your garden next year with the same disease.

Removing Supports

After the plants have been removed from the garden rows, remove any materials that were used for supporting your plants such as cages and trellises. Remove all decaying vines or branches that have attached to the wires and any leftover materials used for tying up the branches.

If you are planning to re-use the same supports from this year's garden for next year, you will want to clean the supports prior to storing them for the winter. Wipe them down with bleach or alcohol towelettes. You could also spray them down with a two-to-one solution of water and bleach. This will kill any diseases that may be lingering on the supports, preventing them from entering the garden next year.

Clean Up Your Rows

Once all the plants and supports have been removed from the garden, it is time to focus your energy on cleaning out the old, dead plant material and any fallen fruit that has been left in the growing rows.

It is important to remove remnant branches and leaves that have fallen into the growing rows to prevent any unwanted disease or pests from entering the garden soil. After all the plants have been removed, it will be difficult to determine whether or not these items died from disease, pest damage or simply of old age. It is best to discard these materials away from your compost bin to prevent the introduction of unwanted diseases to your compost.

Remove any fallen fruit and vegetables that have ended up in your growing rows. As they begin to decay, their seeds will enter into the soil and produce unwanted plants in the growing rows next year. By removing them now, you will save a lot of time and energy eliminating volunteer growth plants in next year's garden.

Now that the summer garden has been cleared, it is time to plant crops that can make it through the winter for an early spring and summer harvest.

CROPS TO PLANT IN THE FALL TO OVER-WINTER FOR A SPRING CROP

Maximize your garden's potential by planting crops in mid to late fall for an early spring and summer harvest.

Fall is the ideal time to plant a few vegetables in your Raised Row Garden that will over-winter right in the elevated soil beds. Crops planted during the fall have the advantage, compared to summer crops, of fewer pests and a more consistent cool and moist soil that allows for good seed germination.

The type of vegetable plants that can tolerate the winter weather and continue to grow into the spring depends on where you live.

In extremely hot climates that have mild winters with little to no chance of freezing temperatures, the winter is the only time that cool-loving crops can be planted and thrive.

However, in cooler climates that have a chance of snow and freezing temperatures, there are a few plants that can be planted in the fall that, after going dormant for the winter, will emerge stronger in the spring. These crops will be larger and taste better than the same varieties planted in the spring.

The advantage of using the Raised Row Gardening system for over-winter crops is three-fold. First, the raised beds allow for the temperatures in the soil to remain warmer than if placed directly in the ground. Second, the layers of the raised rows also allow for adequate drainage of root and bulb crops, which in turn helps to prevent root rot. Third, the mulching system will not only eliminate weeds, but will also provide an added layer of protection to the plants over winter.

Here are some common over–winter crops that can survive the harsh winters in cool environments.

Garlic is one of the few crops that can be planted in the fall, and over-wintered for an early summer harvest.

Garlic

Garlic grows best when planted in the fall. Plant individual garlic cloves in three evenly spaced furrows at a depth of 3 inches (7.5 cm) with the cloves spaced 4 inches (10 cm) apart. This allows the garlic leaves to emerge from the ground and grow 3 to 4 inches (7.5 to 10 cm) in height before the first hard freeze. Mulch the beds with a 4- to 6-inch (10- to 15- cm) thick layer of straw or shredded leaves when the leaves turn brown. In the spring, as cool crops are being planted, the garlic will begin to grow again. The garlic growth will be much faster and stronger than if you planted garlic in the spring.

Garlic will be ready to harvest in early summer, when half of the leaves have turned brown and died off. It is important to save the best garlic bulbs to use as garlic seed in the fall. By using your own garlic seed each year you increase the quality and size of your garlic harvest.

Onions

If you live in mild or cool climates, fall is the time to plant onions. In cold climates, onions can be over-wintered, but will need extra mulch protection as compared to garlic. Plant onion sets in the raised rows at the same time that garlic is planted. Plant in three furrows at a depth of 2 inches (5 cm), spaced 3 inches (7.5 cm) apart. Once the leaves are 2 inches (5 cm) above the ground, add a 2-inch (5-cm) layer of mulch, leaving only the tips of the onions exposed. As they continue to grow in the fall, add more straw or shredded leaves to protect the onions from a potentially harsh winter. Onions should have a full 6 inches (15 cm) of mulch prior to winter's full fury. Like garlic, onions will be ready for harvest in late spring and early summer. The over-wintered onions will be larger and taste sweeter than onion sets planted in the spring.

Root Crops

Although many root crops such as beets and carrots can be planted in the winter in warm climates, there are a couple of varieties, such as Napoli carrots and Lutz Winter Keeper beets that can survive the winter months in cooler climates as well. Be sure to match up your growing zone with the winter hardiness of the varieties that you will be planting. This information can easily be found on the back of most seed packets.

The key to over-wintering root crops is to get them in the raised rows and growing before the first hard frost. It is best to plant them 30 days before the first frost to promote strong enough growth to survive the cold winter months. Mulch the beds with a 4- to 6-inch (10- to 15- cm) thick layer of straw or shredded leaves for added protection over the cold winter months. As the temperatures begin to rise in the spring, both the beet and carrot leaves will continue to grow. Harvest early in the spring, before they send up their flower stalks, to prevent bitter-tasting vegetables. Spring harvested beets and carrots are more tender and sweeter than their fall counterparts.

PUTTING THE RAISED ROW GARDEN TO BED IN WINTER

As autumn fades and the crisp, cool temperatures of fall start to pass, it's time to prepare the Raised Row Garden for the long winter ahead. This is the time of the year that a Raised Row Garden provides crucial nutrients back into the garden and improves the soil in preparation for next year's crops. With just a few simple, low-maintenance chores, you will protect your garden throughout the winter and help to power its growth the following spring.

This requires clearing out the remaining spent and dying annual vegetable plants, covering growing rows with organic materials or planted cover crops and adding additional protection for the over-winter crops like garlic and onions once they begin to emerge through the ground.

As you head into winter, everything should be covered and protected. There should be no bare soil exposed through the winter months.

CLEAR OUT DYING AND DECAYING PLANTS

The first step in preparing your garden for winter is to clear out the remaining dying and decaying plants that were planted for a fall harvest or have continued to flourish past the first frost. Although the process of clearing out the garden began back in the fall, if not during the summer, it will continue to be a necessity until the last plant has died off.

As the fall garden plants begin to die, and the harvest of that plant comes to an end, it is important to remove that plant from the ground as soon as possible. Plants left in the garden past their prime not only become an eyesore, but also an open invitation for pests and disease take hold before the winter cold arrives. Many insects will lay their larvae in the roots and soil around the base of plants that begin to weaken as they start to die off. Removing these plants as soon as they stop producing or begin to fade helps to eliminate potential problems for next year's garden.

As with the summer garden, another important reason to remove non-producing plants is that if decaying vegetables are left on the stems, they will begin to drop their seeds in the rows below, creating an onslaught of volunteer plants the following year. This creates a weeding nightmare in next year's garden.

TO COMPOST OR NOT?

Can I compost my vegetable plants? This is one of the most common questions that gardeners who make their own compost ask. We do compost many of the plants and foliage from our vegetable garden, but with a few, very important exceptions.

Plants that have obvious signs of disease, such as mildew spots or blight, should never be put in compost bins. In addition, we avoid placing heavily laden seed cores from produce such as tomatoes and peppers in our pile.

Composting may not kill all the seeds from the fruits and vegetables in your compost pile. This creates the likelihood of random vegetable plants popping up in unwanted areas throughout your raised rows. Composting diseased vegetable plants can also spread disease damage in next year's garden. Many diseases can survive the composting process and pass on the unwanted plant or soil illness to next year's garden.

The best solution if you want to add these questionable portions of plants to your garden is to burn them in a separate area, and add the ashes to the compost bin. This will ensure that all seeds and diseases have been destroyed and will not be a worry when added to your compost.

COVER YOUR GROWING ROWS WITH ORGANIC MATERIALS OR COVER CROPS

Once your final plants have been removed from the growing rows, it's time to get that cover crop planted!

A cover crop is the planting of legumes or grains such as clover, vetch, annual rye, buckwheat and more that are designed to protect the soil and give back valuable soil nutrients, which have been given to the vegetable plants all summer long. Cover crops are also essential in maintaining the soil structure, preventing soil erosion and blocking weed seeds from entering your raised garden rows over the winter months.

Instead of harvesting the crop in the winter or spring, the entire mass of the legume or grain is incorporated back into the soil to add vitality, nutrients and organic matter that will provide for next year's garden.

Benefits of Planting a Cover Crop

ELIMINATES SOIL EROSION

There is nothing more precious than the soil in the growing rows of your Raised Row Garden. Planted cover crops keep soil from being exposed throughout the winter months. Harsh winter rain, snow and winds can whisk away the top layer of your garden row, including the nutrients in the soil. This erosion will leave your garden with far less productive soil next year.

ELIMINATES NEXT YEAR'S WEEDS

In a Raised Row Garden the key to keeping down next year's weeds is planting a cover crop as soon as the last plant has been pulled out of each row. By keeping soil covered in a luscious, thick blanket of a cover crop, blowing weed seeds and those that have been brought in by birds have trouble finding a bare spot of soil to settle in over the winter months. And without bare soil, they can't find a place to germinate next year. A cover crop will significantly decrease the amount of time and labor spent on weed elimination next year.

LOOSENS COMPACTED AND HARDPAN SOILS

The roots of a cover crop dive down below the soil surface and help break up heavy and compact soil, making it easier for next year's crop to develop deep and strong roots. This will lead to better protection against drought, less need for watering and healthier plants.

DECREASED NEED FOR EXPENSIVE FERTILIZER AND PESTICIDES

By improving the fertility of your soil, you will greatly decrease the need to fertilize your plants after planting. Not only will this help you decrease the cost to maintain your garden, but it also means less time and effort spent on unnecessary garden chores. Cover crops attract beneficial insects and repel harmful insects and diseases found in bare soil. This will decrease the need to apply harmful pesticides.

IMPROVED YIELDS

In a Raised Row Garden, cover crops replenish the amount of nitrogen in your garden. Nitrogen is a key growth component of nearly all vegetable plants, and many, like corn and tomatoes, use up a considerable amount to produce a good harvest each year. By planting cover crops in your growing rows, you are helping to fix the nitrogen levels in the soil naturally.

The roots of cover crops, such as annual rye or clover, work to fix the nitrogen in the soil, making it readily available for next year's crops. If you have ever had a garden in the same spot that grew well for the first few years and then slowly started producing less and less, the loss of elements like nitrogen is most likely the culprit. Cover crops will keep the soil recharged for growth, and these added nutrients will result in a healthier and more productive yield in next year's garden.

When and How to Plant a Cover Crop

The best practice for cover crop planting is to not wait until the entire garden is completely free of all vegetable plants. It is best to seed each of your growing rows as soon as the last plant in that specific row has been removed. This will decrease the chance for weed seeds to enter the bare soil and allow the soil rejuvenation process to begin immediately. You will need to plant your cover crop at least four weeks before the first anticipated frost date. This will allow the seeds to germinate and take hold before going dormant in the winter.

Cover crops can be planted right at the surface level of the soil by simply raking back any existing mulch, seeding the growing zone area, and then slightly working the seeds into the soil with a light raking.

To plant, begin by moving back any of the existing mulch on the top of the soil surface. Next, gently rake the soil to loosen the top of the surface. There is no need to disturb the soil with heavy digging or tilling. A simple raking of the top ⅛-inch (0.25-cm) of soil will allow enough space for a cover crop to germinate.

Next, sow a generous amount of seed on the soil of your growing row. This technique is called broadcast seeding. Think of it much like you would if you were sowing grass seed. We use approximately 1 pound (434 grams) of seed for each of our 18-inch (46-cm) wide by 20-foot (6-meter) long raised rows. The more seed that you spread, the thicker the coverage will be.

Using a garden rake, lightly mix the seed into the soil. The seed will not be completely covered by the soil. Slight raking is more than enough to allow for germination. Most seeds will germinate on their own in seven to fourteen days. Watering your cover crop is an excellent way to speed up germination. However, there is no need to water regularly beyond that unless you experience an extended dry period of a few weeks or more.

Page 157 provides a guide of the most commonly used cover crops that are most beneficial in the Raised Row Garden.

Straw is an excellent choice for covering rows that won't be receiving a cover crop. This organic covering prevents erosion of valuable top soil, and helps to prevent blowing and drifting weed seeds from becoming established in barren soil.

Not Every Row Gets a Cover Crop

There are some exceptions to every rule. To eliminate the time and effort that you spend in your garden, and more importantly to decrease the disruption of the soil in the growing rows, there are times when utilizing a cover crop is more difficult and cumbersome than the benefits that it provides.

When planting small seed crops such as lettuce, kale, spinach, carrots and radishes, it is too difficult to dig through the thick layer of the residual cover crops and roots in the early spring. To plant long strips of seeds in a row that has had a cover crop growing all winter, you would need to dig out trenches through the thick roots of the still decaying cover crop, or turn over the entire row to kill off the remaining living mulch. This would expose unnecessary bare soil, making it easy for weeds to find a home. Although both methods work for planting seeds, cover cropping the area the prior fall will actually cause you unnecessary effort and labor.

In the fall, you should decide the location of the spring small seed crop beds in next year's garden. Then, simply avoid planting the living mulch of cover crops in those rows. Instead, you will apply a thick layer of non-growing, organic mulch material directly on top of the growing row. These organic materials, such as straw and leaves, will provide adequate nutrients to replenish the depleted soil, build up the soil structure for ideal planting conditions in the spring and aid in weed suppression by keeping the bare soil covered over winter.

This will allow you to plant your small seed crops in the furrows dug into the raised row soil without fighting a heavy conglomeration of cover crop roots.

Crop rotation (page 171) is vital to the success of your Raised Row Garden. To avoid a multitude of issues, including decreased productivity, decreased yields and an invasion of pests and disease, avoid planting the same crops in the same location year after year.

What Mulch to Use

There's just one thing to keep in mind when mulching and covering seed rows that will not receive a cover crop. To avoid an additional decrease, or even depletion, of nitrogen, you must add a nitrogen product to the bed space.

Ideally, seed beds should receive a 1- to 2-inch (2.5- to 5-cm) layer of compost, followed by a thick 3- to 4-inch (7.5- to 10-cm) layer of straw or shredded leaves to protect the soil below. As the compost breaks down, it recharges the soil for next year's seed crop. This takes the place of what a cover crop would have provided.

If using leaves as the top protective coat over the compost, it is important to use only chopped leaves instead of whole or tightly compacted leaves. During the winter's rain, snow, freeze and thaw, the chopped leaves slowly break down and become part of the soil mix, while reducing weeds to practically zero. Whole leaves, however, can become a compacted, matted mess that will promote mold and fungus on the underside of the leaves. The leaves will end up sticking together, blanketing the raised row, and will require intensive labor in the spring to break up before your raised bed can be planted.

Straw is also a good choice for use as the top coat layer. It is sold by the bale, and when broken down and shaken over your raised row will provide the adequate coverage to prevent weeds from entering the surface. It breaks down fairly quickly and can easily be worked in the spring to plant those small seed crops. As mentioned before, make sure not to use hay! Hay bales contain seeds, which will be a nightmare to maintain in the spring.

You can purchase compost in bags in bulk and even make your own. If compost is not available, there are other nitrogen-based materials that can be substituted.

NITROGEN-BASED ORGANIC MATERIALS

The organic materials listed below can be used in place of compost as the first level of your over-winter mulch in your raised rows. The important thing to remember is that the organic materials that you place in your raised rows need to have some sort of nitrogen to provide vital nutrients back into your soil. These materials, like when using compost, still need to be a covered by a protective top mulch layer such as straw or shredded leaves.

For rows that will not receive a fall cover crop, it is necessary to amend the soil. Here, a 1- to 2-inch (2.5- to 5-cm) layer of compost is shoveled on top of a growing row that will be used for early spring planting.

ALFALFA MEAL

Alfalfa meal contains various nutrients, including phosphorus, nitrogen and potassium. It is very quick to decompose, but the rapid decomposition causes extreme heat in the soil, which can burn fragile plants when applied in the summer months. For use in the winter, rake it into your soil prior to adding your other organic mulch and let it work its magic. The winter application will provide the beneficial nitrogen to your soil without the worry of harming your delicate seeds and plants.

FEATHER MEAL

Feather meal is made up of processed and ground chicken feathers, which provide a high source of nitrogen that is extremely beneficial for your garden beds. The protein in feather meal takes a long time to break down, making it the perfect over-winter source of nitrogen to be added to your organic materials in raised beds. Use according to package directions.

FISH EMULSION

Fish emulsion is mixed with water and can be sprayed onto the soil prior to adding your chosen organic material to your raised rows. You can even apply a second coat of spray a month later if the weather allows. If applied in the early spring months, wait at least 30 days after you spray the fish emulsion mixture to your soil before planting your small seed crops. This will allow adequate time for the soil to absorb the nutrients and prepare for the seeds to be planted.

GRASS CLIPPINGS

Grass clippings are a readily available source of mulch in the fall and can be obtained for free. It is best to obtain clippings from a chemical-free lawn to decrease the possibility of residual chemicals entering your garden soil. Fresh grass clippings are a natural source of nitrogen and are an especially good choice for adding organic materials to a vegetable garden, providing the nitrogen boost required for next year's plants.

LIVESTOCK MANURE

The manure from grass-eating animals contains an abundant amount of nitrogen and organic matter, but it runs the risk of burning plants or giving weed seeds the opportunity to invade your garden when applied directly in the summer months. However, over winter, you can apply un-composted manure directly to your raised rows. While it sits over the long winter months, it breaks down to provide your soil with the rich nitrogen needed to fuel your garden next year. If you don't have your own livestock, local farmers are usually more than happy to allow others to gather up the manure from their farms. You can even purchase bagged manure from many feed and garden stores.

SOYBEAN MEAL

Soybean meal is an organic material commonly used on lawns because it has a slow to medium nitrogen release. The slow release properties make it another great choice for adding nitrogen to your raised rows over the winter.

MULCHING OVER-WINTER CROPS

Of course, seeding a cover crop is not practical in raised rows that are planted with over-winter crops such as garlic or fall onions, or in perennial raised row beds that hold asparagus, rhubarb, blueberries and strawberries.

Although in warmer climates mulching may not be as crucial for the vitality of your over-wintered plants, it is always necessary to provide some mulch to the raised rows prior to winter. Although both garlic and onions can handle several nights of hard frost, the newly planted crops are prone to damage during an early hard freeze and with the inconsistent freeze and thaw cycle of winter. If not properly insulated, damage can occur to their roots, either killing some of the plants or decreasing the productivity of the yield.

For rows that hold garlic and fall onions, be sure that a thick layer of mulch of 4 to 6 inches (10 to 15 cm) of shredded leaves, straw, compost or grass clippings is in place prior to winter. Again, don't mulch with whole leaves, which can mat down the raised bed, smothering crops.

You must also take into consideration the climate in which you live. If you live in an extremely wet climate that is prone to oversaturated crops or soil-borne diseases caused by wet soil, it is best to use lightweight mulch that can easily be removed if the earth below becomes too saturated. However, if you live in an extremely cold area, a thick layer of straw and shredded leaves might be a better choice to provide adequate insulation to tolerate the winter's cold.

Most perennial fruit and vegetable plants can handle temperatures that dip down below 20°F (-7°C) for one to two nights. However, if your temperatures stay below 20°F (-7°C) for greater than two nights, it is time to protect your perennial plants with an additional layer of mulch. Straw and shredded leaves are good options to use in these perennial raised beds as well.

In the spring, remove the layer of mulch once the top 2 to 4 inches (5 to 10 cm) of the soil temperature is consistently at 40°F (5°C). It is important to leave 1 to 2 (2.5 to 5 cm) inches of the mulch to allow the plants to continue to receive some warmth and to prevent bare ground from being exposed to weed seeds. The new growth will begin to emerge in early spring.

So now that all of the winter garden tasks are completed, it is time to rest your hands, feet and soul for the winter. Get inside, order the most recent vegetable seed catalogs and start dreaming of next year's garden as the snow begins to fly.

THE COVER CROP GUIDE FOR THE RAISED ROW GARDEN

All cover crops are not created equal, especially when it comes to choosing the right variety for a Raised Row Garden. We have included this section to help you understand what varieties of cover crops work best with the Raised Row Garden system in certain regions and a few varieties to avoid all together.

ANNUAL OATS *(Avena sativa)*

Annual oats are the preferred cover crop in regions where there is excessive rain and moisture. They help prevent soil erosion while providing organic material back into the soil. They can be planted various times of the season, from late spring to late summer. Although they work well as a single cover crop, they work best when mixed with other cover crops. Common pairings for an annual oat cover crop include radishes, turnips and clover. Annual oats do not tolerate the extreme cold and freezing temperatures of winter. The plants will die off in the winter, so you must plant the seed by late summer to gain the added benefits for soil amendment prior to the winter. As winter approaches and the oats die off, it is best to add an additional layer of organic material, such as straw or shredded leaves to the top of the raised row for winter protection.

To plant annual oats, lightly rake the soil surface of your raised row. Broadcast seeds on top of the soil, and lightly rake the seeds on top of the soil. There is no need to make sure that the seeds are buried. The more seeds you sprinkle on the soil, the thicker the crop will be.

BUCKWHEAT *(Fagopyrum esculentum)*

Buckwheat is an extremely fast-growing broadleaf plant. It is considered a smothering cover crop that deters weed production, suppressing even the most stubborn of weeds such as quackgrass. Buckwheat is a very fast-growing crop that provides organic matter to the soil and prefers cooler temperatures. It matures in six to eight weeks, making it the preferred cover crop choice in raised rows between spring and fall vegetable plantings, or for a late fall planting before the winter weather arrives.

Broadcast buckwheat seeds in your raised rows 45 days before the first annual frost date. The buckwheat will die off over winter, but will provide for enough coverage of decaying organic matter in the raised row to protect it against weed seeds and soil erosion until the spring crops are ready to be planted.

Left: A variety of cover crops can be planted in your Raised Row Garden including: Crimson Clover (top), Hairy Vetch (right), Winter Rye (bottom) and Buckwheat (left).

(continued)

THE COVER CROP GUIDE FOR THE RAISED ROW GARDEN (CONTINUED)

CRIMSON CLOVER *(Trifolium incarnatum)*

Crimson clover is a legume cover crop that grows well in well-drained soil. You can use it for either a summer cover crop, between spring and fall vegetable plants, or as an over-winter cover crop. For use at the end of the growing season, seed six to eight weeks before the first frost date. Crimson clover will die off in the winter in colder climates, so it is important to get it in the ground as soon as the last plant is pulled out of the raised row. If it begins to grow again in the spring, mow it close to the ground and plant through the dying-off foliage.

Crimson clover and red clover are commonly misunderstood to be the same plant. Unlike red clover, crimson clover is a winter annual. The leaves and stems resemble red clover; however, the crimson clover leaves are more rounded and produce more hair than red clover. If left to flower, which isn't desirable when used as a garden cover crop, you would notice a difference in the size and formation of the blooms. While red clover has a sphere of flowers, the crimson rosette forms in an oblong, cone shape.

As with any cover crop that comes back in the spring, mow off any residual growth prior to planting the vegetable crops directly through the dying foliage.

HAIRY VETCH *(Vicia villosa)*

Hairy vetch is a popular legume cover crop and is commonly used in vegetable gardens due to its strong nitrogen base. Hairy vetch is a good cover crop choice in cold climates and in climates that have an unpredictable amount of rainfall. It is extremely resilient in dry conditions and can thrive when planted in dry zones. It also does well in soil with high pH levels, where it is difficult to grow red clover and alfalfa. Hairy vetch does not prefer to be planted in areas where excessive moisture is an issue. Plant hairy vetch in late summer or early fall, as soon as the last crop has been taken out of the raised row. Broadcast the seeds across the soil surface and rake into the dirt no deeper than ½ inch (1 cm). The crop will begin to grow prior to the winter freeze and will become dormant. In the spring, the growth will reemerge. Cut it back using a push lawnmower prior to it going to seed, or when it becomes greater than 6 inches (15 cm) in height. Mow it down one last time prior to planting your vegetables directly in the resultant organic mulch.

MUSTARD *(Guillenia flavescens)*

The use of mustard as a cover crop has become popular in backyard gardens, not only because mustard is a fast-growing, weed-suppression crop, but primarily because of the suppression of various soil-borne pests and diseases. It is most beneficial to plant mustard seed in raised rows that have contained onions, lettuce and potatoes in the previous garden season.

Broadcast the seeds at a depth of ½ inch (1 cm) five to six weeks prior to the first frost date. A mustard cover crop should provide 100 percent coverage in the raised row. It will die in the winter, and your raised row will be ready for planting in the spring.

RAPESEED *(Brassica napus)*

Rapeseed is a member of the Brassica family and is one of the most versatile cover crops. Not only will rapeseed provide organic matter back into the soil, but it also suppresses weeds, loosens compacted soil and deters pests. It produces a long taproot and small crown roots that will work the soil at various depths.

It can be used as a spring or summer seeded cover crop or planted in the fall as an over-winter cover crop. Broadcast your seeds and lightly rake onto the surface of the soil, making sure the seeds are deeply covered. Rapeseed grows 3 to 5 feet (1 to 1.5 meters) tall and will die off in the winter in cold environments.

RED CLOVER *(Trifolium pratense)*

Red clover is a legume-based cover crop that can be incorporated directly on top of the raised row surface, even when your vegetable plants have yet to be pulled out of the ground. It is slow to germinate, so if you are using it as an over-winter cover crop it should be planted at least six weeks before a heavy freeze for it to become established before the harsh winter arrives. To plant, broadcast the seeds on top of your raised row, and lightly rake the seeds on top of the soil. The red clover will begin to emerge in the late fall. In the spring, it will re-emerge, so cut the red clover with a push lawn mower and leave clippings in the raised row for a continued source of nitrogen. It is most beneficial not to disturb the roots of the clover until mid-May to allow the maximum amount of nitrogen to be provided into the soil. Cut the clover back one last time before planting your summer crops.

(continued)

THE COVER CROP GUIDE FOR THE RAISED ROW GARDEN (CONTINUED)

Red clover is considered a short-life perennial and can live for up to two years in warmer climates. If the clover has made it through the winter and continues to grow, it may be used as living mulch in your growing row zones during the garden season. When it is time to place your plants in the rows, increase your planting zone to a 12-inch (30-cm) wide area to allow your plant to become established in the soil and not be smothered by the fast-growing summer clover. This will allow time for your vegetables to begin to grow, without competing for vital root space in the first few weeks after being transplanted to the garden.

At this time, adding additional mulch such as shredded straw and leaves to the growing row zone is optional. If the clover is thick enough that nothing can penetrate through it to get to the growing row zone soil, then no additional mulch is necessary. However, if the red clover growth is sporadic, then a 3-inch (7.5-cm) layer of shredded leaves or straw is beneficial.

Caution—make sure that you use red clover and not white clover for your cover crop! White clover is a long-term, perennial cover crop that will continue to grow for several years. Although it provides for great weed control in large farm fields, it is considered too cumbersome for the backyard garden.

SUDANGRASS *(Sorghum bicolor* ssp. *drummondii)*

Sudangrass is a short-term cover crop that typically grows to maturity in eight to ten weeks. It does well in heat- and drought-prone areas. Sudangrass provides a large root mass, which is useful in increasing organic soil matter. It is an excellent weed suppressor and is most often used as a cover crop between spring and fall crops. Mow this cover crop when it grows to 8 inches (20 cm) in height to keep the cover crop manageable throughout the season. Cover crop planting for the fall should take place before August 1, as the sundangrass will die over winter. As winter approaches and the crop dies off, it is best to add an additional layer of organic material, such as straw or shredded leaves, to the top of the raised row for winter protection.

TILLAGE RADISH *(Raphanus sativus)*

Tillage radish, also known as the Daikon radish, is a terrific cover crop to decrease soil compaction, improve soil drainage and suppress fall and winter weeds from entering raised rows. When planted in the late summer, the radish tubers will grow deep into the soil, soaking up the nutrients that can be washed away during the winter.

It is important to allow enough time for the radishes to grow in the fall, but do not plant so early that the radish goes to seed. Approximately four to six weeks before the first frost date, broadcast the seed and cover with ½ inch (1 cm) of soil for best germination results. Once the first hard frost date occurs, the radish foliage will begin to die off. Keep the radishes in the ground over winter, as they will begin to decay and provide the stored nutrients back into the soil by the spring. By the time that planting season arrives, the tillage radishes will have decomposed and your soil will be ready for planting.

If tillage radishes are planted in warmer climates and remerge in the spring, cut off foliage prior to the plant going to seed, and allow the radishes to decompose through the spring months. Corn is a terrific succession crop in raised rows that have been over-wintered with tillage radishes.

TURNIPS *(Brassica rapa)*

Similar to tillage radishes, turnips provide several benefits when used as a cover crop. Not only do they loosen compacted soil, turnips improve soil aeration, take in valuable soil nutrients and suppress weeds. Turnips will absorb nutrients in the soil and, when allowed to die off over winter, they will release the nutrients back into the soil for use by the succession planted crop.

Although turnips can withstand some frost temperatures, they should be planted in the fall to allow for adequate growth before winter freeze occurs. Plant the seeds at ½-inch (1-cm) depth, 3 inches (7.5 cm) apart, across your entire raised row.

Allow the turnip roots to remain in the ground over winter and into the spring. This will allow them to decay prior to planting your spring and summer crops.

WINTER RYE *(Secale cereale)*

Winter rye is an excellent choice as an over-wintering cover crop for the Raised Row Garden. It is an annual grain seed that is quick to germinate and therefore more effective at controlling weeds than legume cover crops. The extremely heavy and dense coat that emerges from winter rye seeds completely smothers out competing weed seeds. The root structure of winter rye is only a few inches deep, but contains an extensive network that provides a tremendous amount of nitrogen to the soil.

To plant winter rye, lightly rake the soil surface of your raised row. Broadcast seeds on top of the soil and rake the seeds gently on top of the soil. There is no need to make sure that the seeds are buried. The more seeds you sprinkle on the soil, the thicker the crop will be.

(continued)

THE COVER CROP GUIDE FOR THE RAISED ROW GARDEN (CONTINUED)

Once planted as an over-winter cover crop, the winter rye seeds will germinate and begin to grow before the hard freezes of winter allows the rye to go dormant. In the early spring, the winter rye planted in the raised rows will reemerge and begin to grow.

When planted as a cover crop in the vegetable garden, winter rye should never be allowed to go to seed. If you plant too early or have unusually warm temperatures after planting your seed, the rye may begin to grow at a rapid rate. If the rye grows greater than 6 inches (15 cm) in height, mow off your crop to keep it from going to seed. The clippings from the winter rye cutting should be left in the raised row, as they will decompose and continue to provide beneficial organic materials to the growing row.

As spring progresses and the winter rye begins to grow tall, use a push lawnmower to cut the grass, leaving the clippings in the raised row. A lawn mower bagger can also be used to collect the clippings, which then can be placed in the compost bin. You will need to cut the winter rye three to four times prior to it dying off and leaving the soil ready for planting. Annual, over-wintered cover crops will naturally die on their own as the spring progresses. However, be sure to not let the crop grow large enough to develop seeds, as it will reseed itself in your growing rows.

When it comes time to plant your vegetables, the majority of the rye will have begun to die off and turn brown. However, there will be a few blades of winter rye that will remain green when it is time to plant. It is okay to plant in your designated areas, no matter the condition of your winter rye.

After planting, add your growing row zone mulch to deter any further growth of the cover crop. Over the first several weeks during the growing season, simply pick off any straggling annual rye shoots that emerge from below, before they get large enough to go to seed.

COMMON COVER CROPS TO AVOID IN A RAISED ROW GARDEN BED

Alfalfa

Alfalfa is a cool-loving perennial cover crop that is typically used in large farm fields as a companion crop. It is a great weed suppressor and develops long roots that break up the soil under the ground, promoting good drainage and root expansion for its companion crop.

However, because the Raised Row Garden method promotes a no-till philosophy, it would be extremely difficult to terminate the alfalfa growth without turning over the ground in the spring. Instead of disturbing the soil and causing hours of backbreaking work, it is best to either use a different cover crop than alfalfa or simply dress your raised bed in organic matter with a nitrogen-based material prior to winter.

Dutch White Clover

Dutch white clover is a slow-growing perennial cover crop that will return year after year. It can be grown in wet conditions and is the crop of choice when a dense, compacted area of a cover crop is needed.

Although this perennial cover crop is not recommended for use in the actual Raised Row Garden bed, it can be planted as the material used in the walking zones of your garden. This is an option when straw or shredded bark is not easily available. This is a low-growing cover crop that holds up well to high-traffic areas when densely seeded. Just mow the cover crop off close to the ground to prevent the plants from going to seed and depositing unwanted seedlings in your growing rows.

Perennial Rye

Just like the name implies, perennial rye will continue to grow year after year when planted. Although this has been a great choice for use in large pasture fields for livestock to forage, or as an added mixture to lawn seed, it generally should be avoided for use as a cover crop in the backyard garden.

When established, perennial rye grass can remain productive for up to four years unless affected by an extremely cold winter. This growth would impede the productivity and ability for crop rotation that is necessary in the Raised Row Garden system.

RAISED ROW GARDENING YEAR TWO AND BEYOND

With the first year completed, the simplicity, ease of maintenance and powerful soil-enhancing properties of a Raised Row Garden will continue to take shape in year two and beyond.

Now that the garden rows have been built, planted and amended with organic materials, the workload for the gardener will plummet, while soil fertility and plant productivity will soar!

In year one, the early efforts were focused on building your raised rows by layering topsoil with the organic materials below. Now that those raised rows have been built and have been amended with either a cover crop or organic matter, you will never have to repeat the initial task of building your raised rows in the spring.

In addition, planting can easily be accomplished without turning over the cover crops planted the previous fall. As you will learn later in this chapter, that chore is accomplished by planting right through the decaying and nutrient-supplying cover crops after they are mowed off. And because you layered the garden rows that will host small seed crops, your workload just got that much easier!

THE LOOK OF AN ESTABLISHED RAISED ROW GARDEN—EARLY SPRING

Throughout winter, a Raised Row Garden, much like any type of garden, is in a complete state of dormancy. Over-wintering crops like onions and garlic go dormant with winter's chill and wait for the warmth of spring to renew their growth.

One big advantage of the Raised Row Garden is that, in the winter, every square inch of soil is covered and protected. Not only does this prevent soil erosion and weed suppression, it also allows the gardener early access to the garden in the spring. The walking rows have been covered in mulch and can be utilized at any time, and the growing rows have been protected and can be worked as soon as the ground thaws.

At a time when most traditional gardeners and gardens are at the whim and wrath of Mother Nature, an existing Raised Row Garden in early spring is quite simply immune to most of her challenges. The usual explosion of weeds that can be found in bare soil gardens is all but non-existent in the mulch- and cover-crop protected Raised Row Garden. And with that protection, there is never a need to worry about being able to work the soil after the days and days of rain that the spring can deliver.

All walking rows should have a heavy 4- to 6-inch (10- to 15-cm) thick mulching of wood chips, bark chips, leaves, straw or other organic material already in place from the previous fall chores of putting the garden to bed. This covering is crucial in keeping weeds completely out of all non-growing spaces in the garden.

For the first few years following your initial garden year, you will need to add additional mulch to the walking rows as the materials begin to break down. However, as each season progresses and each year passes, you will need to add less and less. You will also begin to notice that the weeds are all but eliminated. If properly mulched, by year four of the Raised Row Garden, the few weeds that emerge in the walking rows will take less than five minutes a week to remove.

The growing rows, meanwhile, will either be sporting a thick coat of an over-winter annual cover crop, or will be layered with a covering of organic matter and mulch such as shredded leaves and straw.

It is the combination of utilizing a cover crop and providing small seed beds with a thick layer of organic material prior to the start of winter that protects, enriches and continually builds soil fertility in the 18-inch (46-cm) wide growing rows.

Much like each successive year of mulching helps to eliminate weeds in your walking rows, each additional year of growing cover crops or providing organic material in the growing rows will help to increase soil fertility and structure.

MAINTENANCE OF AN ESTABLISHED RAISED ROW GARDEN—EARLY SPRING

In the first month of spring, while traditional gardeners are attempting to start their tillers in preparation for hours of pre-planting work, a Raised Row gardener must concern themselves with just two basic chores, maintaining the walking rows and mowing off over-winter cover crops.

Walking Row Maintenance

The first chore is to take a stroll through your walking rows to check on the condition of your walking row mulch.

It is important to keep a 4- to 6-inch (10- to 15-cm) layer of mulch in the walking rows to eliminate any threat of weeds that may try to develop in the early spring months. Depending on the material that you used as your original walking row mulch, you may or may not need to add additional mulch early in the spring to maintain a thick, protective weed barrier. Some mulch breaks down and decomposes more quickly than other mulches, so adding an additional layer may not be necessary at all.

Because nothing will ever be grown in this space, there is no need to wait for the soil temperature to warm up before adding mulch. You can add additional mulch to your walking rows whenever needed.

As discussed previously, it is important to remember to never rake or turn over existing mulch in the garden, only add new layers as the old layers decay. Although the walking row mulch may look old and tired, turning and raking it has much of the same effect as tilling or digging in the soil—it plants weed seeds that sit on top of the mulch waiting to find a home.

Mowing Off Over-Winter Cover Crop Rows

The growing rows that were planted in a cover crop grew thick, green and heavy throughout the late stages of fall, and then slowly tapered off to a dull, yellowish-green tangled mass of growth through the winter months. Although dormant through wintertime, that thick growth held onto the valuable topsoil in the growing row and kept it from eroding. It also protected the surface from blowing and drifting weed seeds looking for a place to land for spring sprouting.

As temperatures begin to warm in early spring, the first sign of true life in the garden will come from your over-winter cover crops slowly coming back to life. Even if considered annual crops, some cover crops, like annual rye, spring back to life in early spring, before dying back as the season progresses into the latter stages of late spring and early summer.

As the cover crop begins to grow again, it must be prevented from going to seed. The best way to accomplish this task is to mow it down with a standard, push-style lawn mower. With the growing rows set at 18 inches (46 cm) in width, a standard 20- to 22-inch (51- to 56-cm) wide push-mower can quickly mow off each row in a single pass.

Start mowing once the cover crop reaches a height between 4 to 6 inches (10 to 15 cm). Set the deck of your push-mower to the maximum height allowable before mowing off each row. Keeping the cover crop cut at the highest setting possible keeps the soil below protected from any weed seeds that might be blown or brought in as spring progresses.

If your mower comes with a bagging attachment, use it to collect the cover crop cuttings and add them into your compost pile. Cover crop clippings are an excellent material to add to spring compost piles. They are full of nutrients, and their "green nature" helps to heat up piles and get them cooking quickly. If your mower does not have a bagger, simply mow the clippings right back into the rows, providing the continued nutrients right into your growing rows.

The push-mower option is by far the quickest and easiest solution for cutting your cover crops. However, if you are without a push mower, you can also cut the growing cover crop with a string trimmer, hand shears or even a sharp pair of hedge clippers.

Each time that 4 to 6 inches (10 to 15 cm) of new growth develops on the top of your cover crops, continue the process of mowing it down. The frequency required will be dependent on where you live. In warmer climates, you may be required to mow back your cover crop once or twice a week. However, in cooler climates, mowing may only need to be done three or four times before the summer garden can be planted. With each successive mowing, you will notice that the cover crop will begin to slowly die back with less new growth emerging from the ground. The once luscious, thick, green cover crop will now begin to turn brown and start to decompose.

On planting day, mow your cover crop one final time at the lowest height setting of your push mower. You will plant directly through the remnants of the dead cover crop material. Add mulch to the growing row zone as you did in year one after planting. As the growing season progresses, the cover crop will continue to decompose and provide additional nutrients to the soil. This truly no-till gardening method makes the Raised Row Garden simply amazing for year two and beyond.

CROP ROTATION

Crop rotation, at its very core, is the simple practice of growing plants in a different location of the garden each year.

If you continue to plant the same type of vegetable plant in the same space year after year, the health and productivity of your plants will suffer with each successive planting.

Vegetable plants devour a tremendous amount of minerals and nutrients from the soil in which they are grown. By replanting vegetables in the same space, the soil becomes depleted of those invaluable resources, and vegetable plants and yields suffer. By moving your plants to a new raised row from year to year, you give the soil a chance to recover from the same plant taking out the same nutrients.

Different crops use up different nutrients in the soil when compared to other crops. Corn and tomatoes are heavy nitrogen feeders that quickly deplete nitrogen in the soil. If you plant corn or tomatoes in the same spot year after year, that soil will begin to be depleted of nitrogen. By changing the location of these crops each year, you will balance out the soil's available nutrients.

CROP ROTATION SAMPLE PLAN

Year 1

Crop rotation is a huge key to keeping a garden productive and healthy year after year. Ideally, the same vegetables should never be grown in the same row in successive years. By using a quadrant system with 4 designated zones of growing rows, you can rotate similar crops into a new zone each year for 3 successive years.

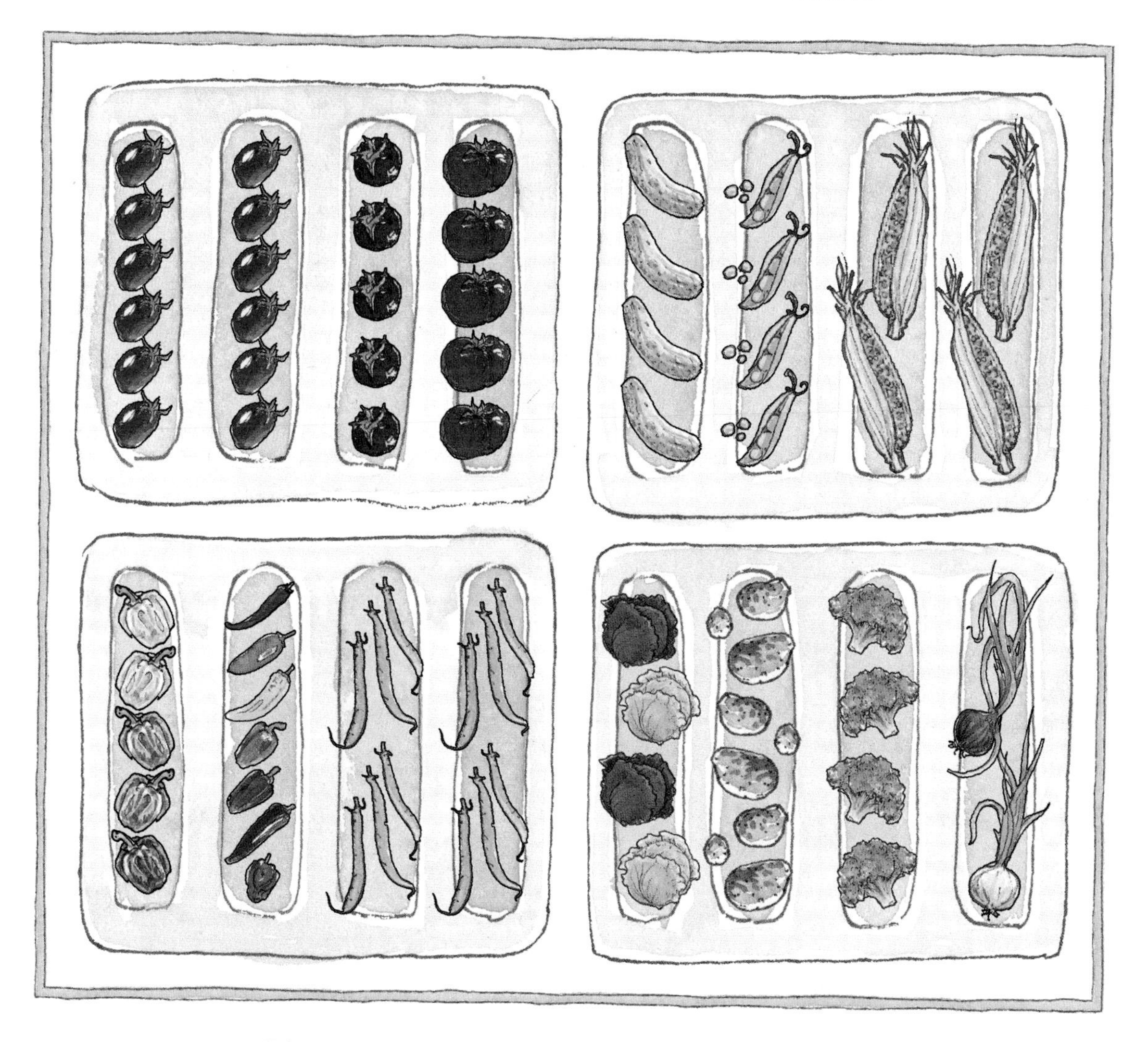

CROP ROTATION SAMPLE PLAN

Year 2

In year 2, note how each prior year's zone is planted and moved into a new quadrant using a clockwise rotation.

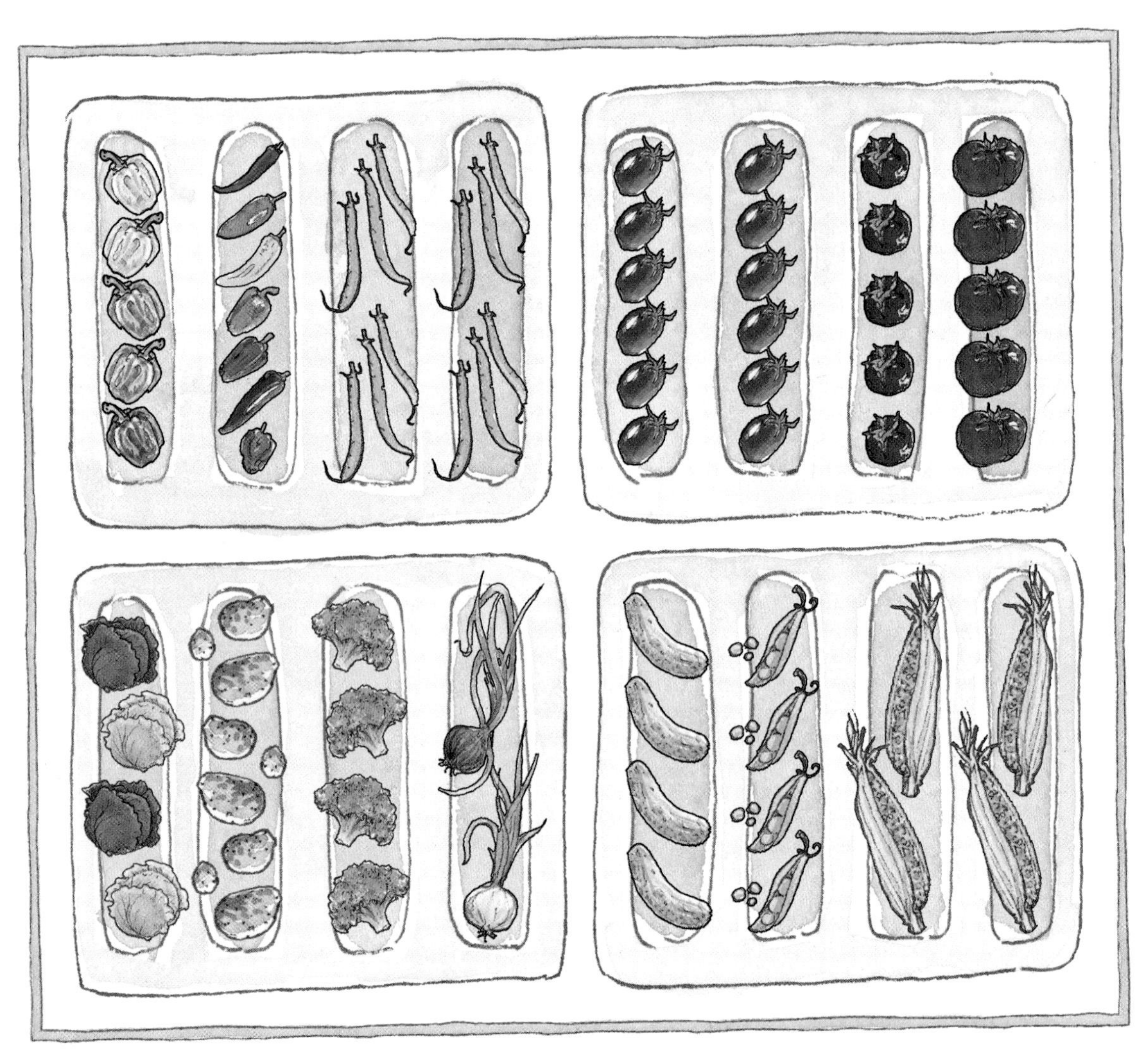

CROP ROTATION SAMPLE PLAN

Year 3

In year 3, the quadrants shift clockwise again to a new growing space.

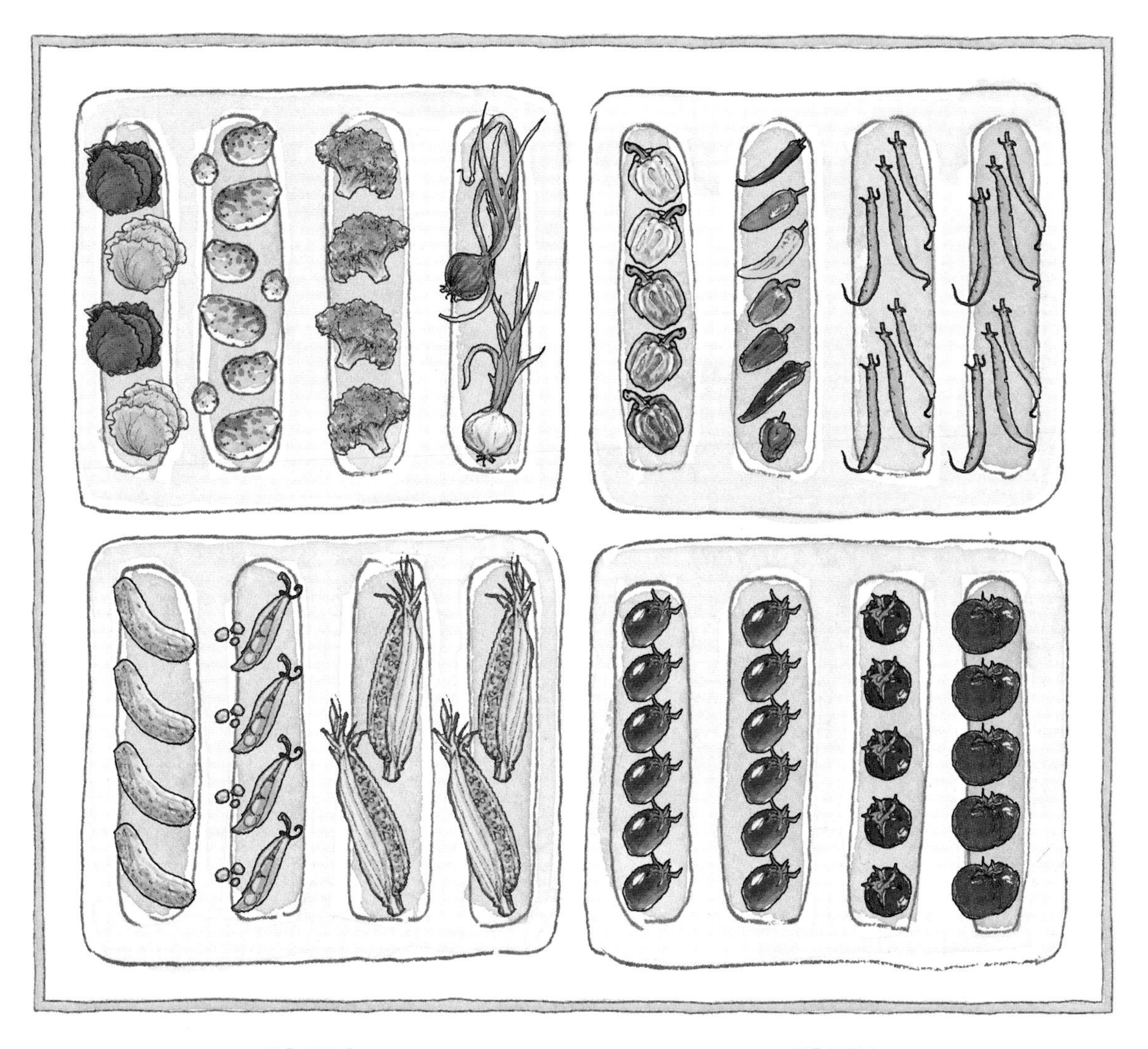

CROP ROTATION SAMPLE PLAN

Year 4

By year 4, each quadrant of similar crops has been grown in every section of the garden. As year 5 ensues, the plants will head back into their first year's placement. This long-term rotation allows soil to recover the specific nutrients that each crop requires.

ZONE 2 ZONE 3

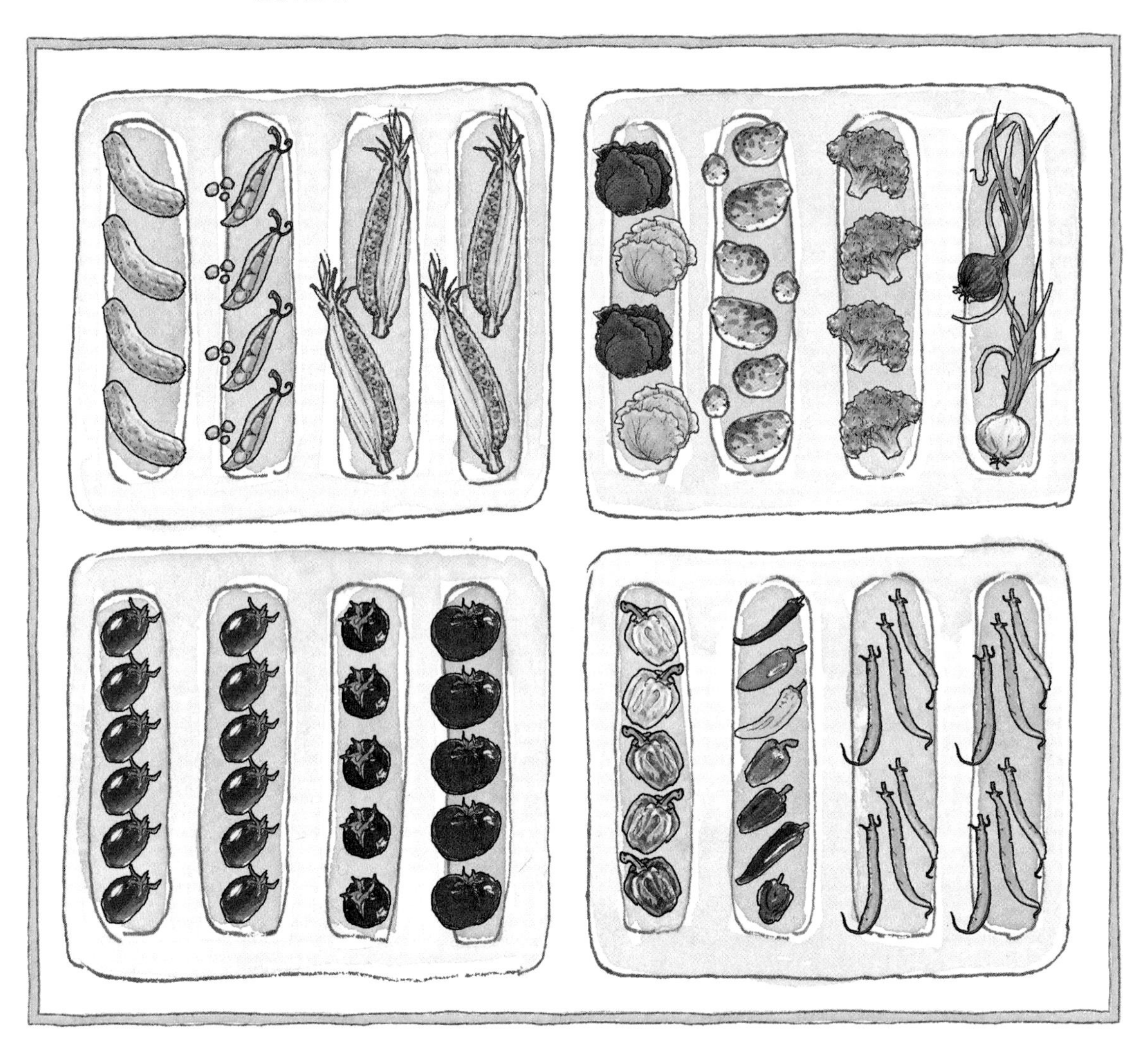

ZONE 1 ZONE 4

But crop rotation helps solve more than just soil deficiencies. Both soil-borne disease and unwanted pests have a much easier time becoming established when similar plants are grown in the same spot each year. When the same plants are grown in the same location again and again, pests and disease don't need to search for their preferred host. They remain in the ground and become a stronger, bigger threat to your plants each year. Fungi, root-rot, damping off and bacterial wilt are all common soil-borne diseases that can take hold, and sit waiting to destroy the next season's crop when it is planted in the same space.

In a Raised Row Garden, crop rotation means alternating crops at least every year so that the same vegetable plant will not be grown in the same space as the previous year.

Remember from Chapter 3, when you created your initial Master Garden Plan (page 37), that it's helpful to group similar types of plants together in the same row, or next to each other in different rows. The four basic categories are leafy cops, fruiting crops, root crops and legumes.

Every year, rotate each group of plantings so they move to where another group grew the season before. It is easiest to rotate them in a clockwise direction until all other groups move over a full section. Do this each year, and by your fifth garden season, the plants will have returned to where you planted them in your inaugural garden.

SEED CROPS

In the same way it's important to develop a garden plan before you plant your first year's garden, it is just as important to develop the next year's plan before planting fall cover crops. Knowing where you will be planting small, early seed crops such as lettuce, spinach, carrots and radishes in next year's garden will be a factor in your short- and long-term garden plan.

The raised row beds of these small seed crops will not be planted with the fall cover crop this year. That soil will instead get amended with a layer of organic material as discussed in Chapter 9. Planning ahead is crucial to maximize soil amendment without causing you unnecessary labor in next year's garden.

CONTINUING YOUR MASTER GARDEN PLAN

So, now that we know the factors that need to go into a short- and long-term Raised Row Garden, you can continue to develop your Master Garden Plan for years to come.

Depending on how many rows you have in your garden, you can rotate the crops each year on a two, three or four year basis to keep the soil fresh and productive. If you have the space and the rows, rotating crops so that they are not in the same space for at least four years is the absolute best. This, of course, is not always an option. But, at the least, make sure the same crop never gets planted in the same row two years in a row.

Always keep a record of where plants grew, and how well they did there—what problems you had with pests or disease, and solutions you might have found to the issues. Keeping all of this information in one place will be invaluable to grow a thriving garden year after year.

You can also determine at this time if the size of your garden is adequate to meet your needs. If you want to grow more of your own food, then this is the time to plan your expansion for next year's garden. Determine how many additional raised rows you need, and begin to build them as you did in your initial garden. Building can be completed in the fall with a fall cover crop planted, or can be completed in the spring. It is important to remember to include these expansion rows in the overall garden plan prior to planting to ensure adequate rotation of the previous year's garden crops.

PEST CONTROL

Now that you know what, if any, pests and soil-borne diseases are present in your garden from your first year's garden experience, there are additional solutions to help control issues that may occur in the coming years. In addition to the natural protection that healthy soil in a Raised Row Garden provides, companion planting and row covers can help protect your plants in advance of known problems.

Companion Planting

As discussed in Chapter 3, certain plants can be planted together or next to each other that bring in natural predators for pests that are harming your plants. Consult the guide on page 60 for more specific information.

Row Covers

Row covers can easily be fashioned over the 18-inch (46-cm) wide growing rows to protect susceptible plants from cabbage worms, moths, beetles and more. The covers can easily be anchored through the mulch layers, providing total protection for affected plants. Reference page 58.

PREPARING TO PLANT YEAR TWO

Unlike in a traditional tilled garden, you can begin planting in a Raised Row Garden as soon as the ground can be worked and it is warm enough for seed germination. Gardeners who use a tiller have to wait until the ground is dry enough to till the soil. And because this process must be repeated over and over again prior to planting, their early spring crops will be delayed when compared to the time frame in which a Raised Row gardener can begin.

Seed Crops

When the ground is warm enough to work, you can begin to plant your early spring crops. The organic materials that covered your small seed beds in the fall have now begun to decay, and you will plant your seeds directly in the amended soil. There is no need to turn over the soil for planting, just furrow out your long strips and plant according to the seed packet instructions or following our planting guide on page 60. The areas in the growing row that are not furrowed for seed do not need to be disturbed at all. The less that you disturb your soil, the less likely weeds and weed seeds can be established.

Once your seed crops have been planted, immediately add compost and mulch as you did in year one.

Transplants

As stated above, before planting your main garden with the traditional transplant vegetables, you need to mow off any growing rows where cover crops have been. Again, use the lowest level the mower will allow to cut the old cover crop growth right to the ground.

With the rows mowed off for the last time, it's now time for planting! You will not be turning the ground over or adding additional straw and soil. Because your Raised Row Garden has been given the nutrients it needs through the cover crop, you will plant directly through the organic material and right into the soil below.

Prior to planting, mark off where each planting zone will be in each growing row. This can be done by placing individually-potted plants directly on top of the growing row, or even with a rock that is nearby.

Once you have marked off where plants will go, it is time to drive your support systems in place. As in the first year, it is much easier to put the supports in place before planting, and also eliminates the worry of hitting or disturbing the root systems of vegetable plants later on.

Once your supports are in place, it's time to plant. And, it couldn't be simpler!

Use that same standard post hole digger you used in year one to create a 6- by 8-inch (15- by 20-cm) hole. Drive the post hole digger directly into the space where you will be planting. In just a few seconds, you can easily create a 6- to 8-inch (15- by 20-cm) deep planting hole right through the cover crop roots and into the soil below.

Now, just like in year one, supplement each growing hole with a mixture of compost, eggshells, worm castings and existing soil from the hole. As you put the existing soil back in place, leave any roots of the cover crop on top of the rows to continue to decay.

After the transplant is securely tucked in the soil, apply a 2-inch (5-cm) layer of compost or preferred planting zone mulch 12 inches (30 cm) around each plant.

Finally, mulch the rest of the growing row as you did in year one.

As your Raised Row Garden continues to develop and become established year after year, your soil will become more fertile each season. Meanwhile, weeds will continue to diminish, thanks to the continued mulching practices. The amount of effort and labor that your garden will demand of you will be minimal, and the results will be outstanding!

ACKNOWLEDGMENTS

There is a simple pleasure in gardening that can only be known to those who take up the hobby. Gardeners are a special group of people who willingly and openly share their knowledge, experiences, dos and don'ts and, of course, their tall tales of growing record produce at will. We would be remiss if we didn't first thank every one of the incredible gardeners we have met over the years whose tips, guidance and yes, even tall tales helped shaped our own way of gardening. Without them, *Raised Row Gardening* would never have come to fruition.

To our friends at the Union County Master Gardener's Association, Licking County Master Gardener's Association and the Muskingum Valley Garden Society, we thank all of you for allowing us the opportunity to speak to your members and learn from the best!

Beyond our beloved gardening friends, there have been so many others that have made this book turn from a dream into a reality.

To Craig Ratai, our friend, neighbor and personal advisor when it comes all things DIY— we are fairly certain the majority of our garden projects would never come true without your assistance! We thank you from the bottom of our hearts, and we apologize in advance for giving your wife Bev more gardening ideas for you to help with.

To our editor, Sarah Monroe, and the rest of the team at Page Street, what can we say but a Great Big Huge Thank You! Thank you for finding us, for believing in us and for helping to guide two fledgling authors through the entire process of writing a book from cover to cover. Your guidance, suggestions and patience served us well! We both cannot tell you enough how grateful we are to have had the opportunity to work with you.

To Erica Kay, UA Chamberlain and UA Creative Studios, thank you for the incredible photography for the book! We have learned so much from both of you and you are simply a pleasure to work with!

To our four wonderful children, Loryn, Aaron, Wes and Nolan, thank you for tolerating your "crazy" parents throughout the writing of this book. We know you secretly all love to garden!

Most of all, thank you to our parents, Dick and Candy Foehl and William and Rita Competti, for introducing us to all things gardening from an early age!

We might not always have been willing participants in our early childhood years, but by exposing us to the dirt and vegetables at an early age, you planted the seeds for our own love of gardening some 40 years later.

ABOUT THE AUTHORS

In 2010, seeking a way to become responsible for the food on their table and to simplify the typical life of two full time professionals balancing careers and a family, Jim and Mary Competti began Old World Garden Farms.

Starting from scratch, they worked together to convert an overgrown three-acre field into a self-sustaining farm that could feed their family and their souls. Their only requirements were to grow their food without the use of chemicals or pesticides, and above all, keep it simple and fun. In the process, they created their Raised Row Gardening method that has gained popularity across the world as a simple, low-maintenance and, of course, fun way to grow backyard vegetables.

They now grow nearly 75 percent of their own food, raise a small flock of chickens and maintain two bee hives, a small orchard and a vineyard. In the process they have used reclaimed and recycled materials to build everything from their barn, chicken coop, compost bins and more.

In early 2012, they created the website oldworldgardenfarms.com to document the entire process for others looking to do the same. The website has grown in just five short years to over 30 million visitors and 200,000+ followers from over 226 countries around the globe.

In 2016, they published their first book, *Growing Simple*, chronicling the trials and tribulations of creating their homestead.

In addition to their work at the farm, Mary holds a degree from The Ohio State University and works as a pediatric occupational therapist. Jim is a graduate of Ohio Northern University and is Marketing Director for a regional firm based out of Charlotte, North Carolina.

INDEX

H

I

J

K

L

M

N

O

P

Q

R

S

T

V

W

Y

Z

trustees